TABLE OF CONTENTS

Top 20 Test Taking Tips...4
Assessment and Diagnostic Teaching..5
Oral Language and Oral Communication..10
Reading Development...16
Writing and Research..36
Specialized Knowledge and Leadership Skills...44
Practice Test...56
    Practice Questions..56
    Answer Explanations...80
Secret Key #1 - Time is Your Greatest Enemy..93
    Pace Yourself...93
Secret Key #2 - Guessing is not Guesswork...93
    Monkeys Take the Test..93
    $5 Challenge..94
Secret Key #3 - Practice Smarter, Not Harder...94
    Success Strategy..95
Secret Key #4 - Prepare, Don't Procrastinate..95
Secret Key #5 - Test Yourself...96
General Strategies..97
Special Report: What Your Test Score Will Tell You About Your IQ......................................102
Special Report: What is Test Anxiety and How to Overcome It?..104
    Lack of Preparation..104
    Physical Signals...105
    Nervousness...105
    Study Steps..107
    Helpful Techniques...108
Special Report: Retaking the Test: What Are Your Chances at Improving Your Score?.......113
Special Report: Additional Bonus Material...115

Top 20 Test Taking Tips

1. Carefully follow all the test registration procedures
2. Know the test directions, duration, topics, question types, how many questions
3. Setup a flexible study schedule at least 3-4 weeks before test day
4. Study during the time of day you are most alert, relaxed, and stress free
5. Maximize your learning style; visual learner use visual study aids, auditory learner use auditory study aids
6. Focus on your weakest knowledge base
7. Find a study partner to review with and help clarify questions
8. Practice, practice, practice
9. Get a good night's sleep; don't try to cram the night before the test
10. Eat a well balanced meal
11. Know the exact physical location of the testing site; drive the route to the site prior to test day
12. Bring a set of ear plugs; the testing center could be noisy
13. Wear comfortable, loose fitting, layered clothing to the testing center; prepare for it to be either cold or hot during the test
14. Bring at least 2 current forms of ID to the testing center
15. Arrive to the test early; be prepared to wait and be patient
16. Eliminate the obviously wrong answer choices, then guess the first remaining choice
17. Pace yourself; don't rush, but keep working and move on if you get stuck
18. Maintain a positive attitude even if the test is going poorly
19. Keep your first answer unless you are positive it is wrong
20. Check your work, don't make a careless mistake

Assessment and Diagnostic Teaching

Formal assessments

The two main types of formal assessments are norm-referenced and criterion-referenced. Norm-referenced assessments are those that compare a student's scores or achievement to that of his or her peers. Some of the most notable norm-referenced assessments are college entrance exams, such as the ACT and SAT exams. Students do not fail these tests. Instead, they are given a score which is compared to other students to determine where they fall within a group of their peers. Whereas norm-referenced assessments compare one student to others, criterion-referenced assessments are used to show what a student knows and can do. Most state achievement tests are criterion-referenced. Most of the time, these assessments have a set standard that the students are expected to achieve. If students are above these cut lines, they pass; if they are below, they fail.

Overcoming testing disadvantages

Norm-referenced assessments and criterion-referenced assessments both have their advantages and disadvantages. The advantage to norm-referenced assessments is the ability to measure the progress of an individual compared to others. The disadvantage is that these tests cannot measure the progress of the entire group, and they cannot be used to determine if educational reforms are working. On the other hand, criterion-referenced assessments can show group improvement, but don't show how the scores compare to others and whether the test's expectations are too high or too low. However, many tests can be used for both norm-referenced and criterion-referenced assessment. In these cases, it does not matter how the tests are taken or scored, but how they are viewed. For example, the ACT exam shows how students compare to others. But that same test can also be used to show what the students know and in what areas they need improvement.

Informal assessments

Two types of informal assessments are informal reading inventories and anecdotal records. An informal reading inventory is an assessment or survey given by a student's regular teacher to help determine the needs of that student. These inventories usually consist of three parts. The teacher should assess the student before the reading takes place, during the oral presentation, and after the reading for literal and inferential comprehension. Informal reading inventories should not be used alone to determine the instructional needs of a student. Anecdotal records are written records of a student's progress and development over time. This includes social, emotional, physical, and intellectual development. A teacher compiles these records, usually on a day-to-day basis, and notes the specific time and date of each occurrence. Anecdotal records are always kept in a positive tone. They reflect what a student has done and can do, not what they haven't done and cannot do.

Reading levels

The best way for a reading specialist to assess a student's reading levels and plan proper instruction is to administer an informal reading inventory. An informal reading inventory is an assessment given by the teacher and is used to discover an individual's strengths and weaknesses. The student reads aloud specific passages selected by the teacher as the teacher takes notes on his or her performance. The student also is asked comprehension questions after the reading. Reading levels are determined by the percentage of words correctly read and the percentage of comprehension questions correctly answered. After the assessment, the teacher uses those percentages to plan instruction tailored to the student.

Print concepts

One way to assess a child's knowledge of concepts of print is to have the student orally read a simple book or text to you. Even if the child cannot read, "pretend reading" can give insight into his or her knowledge of concepts of print. For example, if he or she holds the book correctly and turns the pages properly, it shows knowledge of how print is organized and that each page carries meaning. The student also may show an understanding of the connection between spoken words and words that are written. This is shown by turning the pages of the book as he or she tells the story. You may also have the student move his or her fingers across the words he or she is "reading." This will help assess the knowledge of the directionality of print. If the student struggles with any of these concepts, then additional instruction may be needed.

Phonemic skills

Students' phonemic awareness skills can be assessed through both written tests and oral tests. Written tests may involve giving the students a list of words. Have them separate each word into individual phonemes. For example, if the written word "cat" appears on the test, students should put lines through the word to show the separation. In this instance, "c/a/t" would be the correct answer. You can also quiz each student verbally. For example, you may ask, "Listen to the word 'sat.' How many sounds do you hear?" Verbal quizzes are also more effective for testing the phonemic awareness skills of blending separate phonemes to form a word and phoneme substitution. For example, you could ask the student, "Listen to these sounds—ta...ble. Together, what word does that make?" This could not be done with a written test. By examining answers from both tests, you will be able to properly assess each student's strengths and in which areas they require help.

Letter recognition

Letter recognition skills can also be assessed through both oral tests and written tests. An example of an oral test would be to write every letter of the alphabet on the board. As you point to each letter, have the student say its name. Written tests are also effective and can save valuable time. Call out the names of letters and have each student write them down on paper. This way saves time because you can test all the students at the same time. With the oral test, you can only test one student at a time. With either test, be sure that you don't only test them in alphabetical order. Some students may only memorize the order of the alphabet and not each individual letter. Therefore, it is important to mix up the order of the letters during testing.

Sound-symbols

One way to assess a child's sound-symbol knowledge is to read aloud a passage and then have the student write down what you said. For example, let's say you are assessing the student's knowledge of the /ch/ sound. Read out loud the sentences, "Chuck likes ch sounds. He likes chocolate." Have the student write these down. If the writing looks something like, "Chuck likes ch sounds. He liks choclate," then the student is showing good awareness of /ch/ sounds. However, if the student writes something like, "Chac lix ch sounds. He lix joclet," then he or she is having problems with phonemic awareness, and more specifically, sound-symbol knowledge involving /ch/ sounds.

Mispronunciations

A student mispronounces the words "one," "some," "come," and "where" when reading out loud. All these words are words that have irregular spellings and must be recognized by the student on sight. They cannot be sounded out or figured out by using phonics. For example, the student may have tried to sound out the word "where" and pronounced it as the word "were." Even if the student corrects himself or herself, the initial misreading of the words shows that he or she needs help with such words. The student would best benefit from a teacher's instruction that would help him or her recognize and memorize these sight words.

Word-attack skills

When assessing students' word-attack skills, it is important to use "psuedowords," or words that resemble real words but in fact have no meaning. This is important because you do not want possible sight words that can simply be recalled by students. While there are many different methods to assess word-attack skills, they all have certain things in common. Unknown words should look like familiar words or at least have groups of letters that are common. Tests should also include questions that have pictures, as using pictures is one method of word-attack strategies. Whichever type of assessment you use, make sure to cover each strategy that you have taught to get a good idea about the effectiveness of the instruction.

Student's vocabulary

A good way to assess a student's vocabulary is through written tests. One such test is a fill-in-the-blank test. Put together a list of sentences that include vocabulary words that the class has studied or should know. Then take out the words and insert blanks for the students to fill in. You can place the vocabulary words in a word bank if you wish. This assessment will also test their knowledge of how the words are used in context. You can then use the results to see which words should be covered further.

Word recognition

Word recognition in context can be assessed in a manner similar to what is used for vocabulary assessment. Complete sentences should be used so that the readers can use the context of surrounding words and sentences to find meaning. Fill-in-the-blank questions can be used, but some find that word choice questions are more effective. For example, a possible sentence could be, "I don't know (where/were) he went." These assessments do differ from vocabulary assessments, however. Word recognition in context assessments should include entire paragraphs, not just single sentences. Also, the volume of unknown words should not be as high. The reason for these differences is that comprehension is more important in word recognition than it is for vocabulary.

Reading fluency

When assessing a student's reading fluency, four components should be addressed. These are reading rate, accuracy, proper expression, and comprehension. Reading rate, or speed, is usually calculated in words per minute. If accuracy is also taken into account, then it is calculated in words correct per minute.

Accuracy is also assessed by how many words were incorrectly identified. You should also make a note of each word that was self-corrected by the student. Expression includes using the appropriate pitch, stress, and pauses while reading. Finally, comprehension should be assessed by asking the student questions after the reading is complete.

Reading comprehension

Many studies have been conducted on the effectiveness of assessing reading comprehension. However, one strategy has been found to be extremely, if not the most, effective. This strategy consists of two parts. First, as the children read, monitor their comprehension by asking them questions, such as who, what, when, where, how, and why. Second, simply ask the students to summarize the text when they are done reading. If they can accomplish those two tasks, then they have most likely comprehended what they read. If not, you have specific areas for needed improvement.

Using spelling tests

Spelling tests are a good way to assess children's reading levels. Comprise a list of 20 words that have a variety of graphemes and spelling features. It is important that the students not study these words in order to get a true assessment of what they know. It is also important that the students know this test is not for a grade, just to find out what they know. Call out the words and use them in a sentence to administer the test. When scoring the test, score each possible spelling feature, not just the entire word. Features can include onsets, rimes, affixes, and so on. If a student is incorrect on one or fewer of the total answers for one specific spelling feature, then that student is doing well. Two or more wrong answers show that those

areas need to be addressed. If a student has incorrect answers for an entire feature, then that concept is beyond them and earlier features need to be addressed first.

Differentiation

The most commonly accepted definition of differentiation is the adjustment of teaching according to the needs of students. This can apply to the entire class, groups, or individual students. While the definition of differentiation is still debated, the most important thing teachers must realize is that is up to them to find the most effective method for them and their students, regardless of what it may mean. Three commonly accepted ways to differentiate instruction for students is by task, by outcome, and by support. When differentiating by task, different tasks are assigned for students of different ability. For example, some students could be given assignments on basic phonetic principles while advanced students are given assignments on more complex principles. When differentiating by outcome, open-ended tasks are given to students. The same tasks are done, but different outcomes are displayed by students of different abilities. When differentiating by support, more help is given to struggling students within the group.

Group reading projects

To organize a group reading project for elementary students, a teacher should divide the students into small, heterogeneous groups. It is important to give the students clear, specific guidelines and rules for the project as well as for their behavior. Goals should also be established to keep the students on track. Each student should have an equal part to play within the group. It is also extremely important to have individual assignments that students can complete if they finish their reading before other members of the group. This way, they will not be distracted or distract others before other group members are ready to move on to the next step of the project.

Flexible groupings

Different groupings can help with students' changing needs. Common groupings include grouping students by number and by ability. Small groups, consisting of four people, create good interaction among students, allowing everyone to get information from each person. Large groups of six to eight students allow different students to do different tasks for the same project. Grouping students with similar skills encourages those who may feel embarrassed by knowing less than other children. Grouping students of different skills allows them to help one another. Better students develop more confidence while students with difficulties get help without being "exposed" to the entire class. There are also "mingle" activities. Mingle activities allow students to interact with the entire class without being "exposed" to the entire class at one time. These activities involve students interacting with many different members of the class within a short time to accomplish the same task. By doing this, students will interact with others at different levels, both stronger and weaker.

Listening strategies

Listening strategies are the techniques used by a teacher to build listening comprehension and recall in students. There are two main classifications—top-down strategies and bottom-up strategies. Top-down strategies are based on the listener. The listener uses background knowledge to interpret the information given. Such strategies include predicting and summarizing. Bottom-up strategies are based on text. The listener relies on how words are used to establish meaning. These strategies include listening for specific details and recognizing word patterns. Oral reading time can be a great way to improve students' listening skills. Before you read to them, tell them they will be asked to give a summary of the story when you are finished. In order to do so, they will have to apply top-down strategies by listening for the main idea. You can also use this to teach bottom-up strategies. Repeat the story again, but before you do, ask them questions concerning specific details. This time when they listen, they will have to use bottom-up strategies in order to hear and remember the specifics.

Oral Language and Oral Communication

Speaking vocabulary

A good way to increase your students' speaking vocabularies is to introduce a "word of the day" program. At the beginning of each day, introduce a word and give its definition. If time permits, have each student say a sentence that includes the new word. You should also encourage them to try to use the word correctly at some point during the school day. If they succeed, then they are rewarded with a sticker, extra credit, or whatever is appropriate for their grade level. By encouraging them to use the word during the course of a normal day, you will be helping them build their speaking vocabulary in a meaningful way.

Communication to inform

It is important to teach students to use oral language for different purposes, such as to inform, to explain, to persuade, and to entertain. To teach them to use language to inform, group the students into pairs. Have each student ask his or her partner a few predetermined questions, such as "Where do you live?" or "How many people are in your family?" After each student gets his or her answers, have each pair go to the front of the room and describe their partners. By doing this, they will learn how they can use oral communication to learn about others and to inform other people about what they learned.

Communication to explain

It is important to teach students to use oral language for different purposes, such as to inform, to explain, to persuade, and

to entertain. To teach them to use language to explain, have each student go to the front of the room and explain something in which they have to use specific details. An example is trying to explain to the class where they live. If they are not comfortable with this, have them choose something similar. In order to give directions, they must use oral communication in a way that other people can understand. If the class is too large to do this one at a time, separate the class into groups and have them explain their directions to one another.

Communication to persuade

It is important to teach students to use oral language for different purposes, such as to inform, to explain, to persuade, and to entertain. To teach them to use language to persuade, separate them into groups. Have each group select a topic that they would like to see changed. For example, one group may choose "why we need a longer recess." Have the groups prepare a presentation to be given in front of the class. In order to make a persuasive argument, they will have to learn to choose their words carefully. It is also important that you set strict ground rules to keep the children in line and on topic.

Communication to entertain

It is important to teach students to use oral language for different purposes, such as to inform, to explain, to persuade, and to entertain. To teach them to use language to entertain, separate them into groups. Have each group create a short play to present to the entire class. Each student should have an equal part. In order to do this successfully, they will have to communicate with each other as well as use each person's creative skills. They will also realize that to present their play in an entertaining manner, they will need to use good word choice and oral communication skills.

Communication to express creativity

It is important for students to develop creativity and to have the ability to express that creativity through oral communication. To accomplish this, read the children a story. Do not read the entire story, though. Stop at an appropriate place and instruct the students to make up their own endings. By doing this, they will have to use their creativity to create an ending and use their oral communication skills to express it. Doing this activity in groups will allow them to share thoughts and ideas. However, it is important that you make sure every student plays an equal role and that each student's ideas are heard.

Word choice

It is vital that you teach students the importance of their choice of words so they can learn to speak effectively through oral communication. One good way to accomplish this is to play a simple game. Hold up a picture of an object. While you do this, have two students sit facing each other. One student should be facing you and the other student should be facing away from you. The student who is facing the picture tries to describe it to the other student in an attempt to get him or her to say the name of the object. They then switch places and repeat the process. Seeing the problem from both sides will educate the students on the importance of word choice. Presenting it as a game helps keep them motivated as well.

Oral and nonverbal communication

In addition to learning to use oral communication, students need to learn how to use nonverbal communication. A simple game can help accomplish this. Divide the class into three groups. Each group will attempt to put together a jigsaw puzzle. There is a catch, however. You will assign each group a nonsense word. This is the only word that they are allowed to say as they put together the puzzle. In order to communicate effectively, they will have to use nonverbal communication, such as gestures. Also, since they have only one word to say, they will learn to vary things such as pitch, rate, and volume. All these are essential when learning to communicate, both verbally and nonverbally.

Correct verb tenses

To help teach students the correct tenses for verbs, separate the class into groups of three. Give a verb, then have a group give the three correct tenses (present, past, past participle). Each student is asked to provide one tense. If all three students answer correctly, the group is awarded one point. Proceed to the next group and do the same thing. At the end of the game, whichever group has the most points wins. Each group member should give their answer without any help. This will force each student to concentrate.

Sentence structure

Oral reading time, or "story time," can be a good opportunity to teach or review sentence structure. As you read the story, occasionally pause to repeat a sentence. Have the students repeat the sentence out loud and then give its structural components (noun, verb, etc.) Begin with simple sentences with simple components. As your teaching progresses and students learn the more complex components, you can move to more difficult and more complex sentences. By tying the structural components to a story, students will have an easier time establishing a relationship between the words and their meaning.

ESL students and reading

When preparing to teach a student who is learning English as a second language, a reading specialist must take into account the student's primary language. The specialist needs to find out the similarities between the sound system of the primary language and the sound system of the English language. Through doing this, he or she can make a positive transfer between the two languages. If certain letters correspond to the same sounds in both languages, the specialist can use these similarities to make the student's reading development much quicker and easier.

Students beginning to learn the English language can feel isolated from their peers. This can cause an incredible barrier for their learning development. If they are taught early how to answer questions about themselves and ask others the same questions, they can feel more included in the learning process, thus improving their development. Learning to answer questions such as "What is your name?" and "Where are you from?" along with basic communication elements create a solid foundation for learning. Not only will they feel more included within the group, they will not feel as bored or lost as they would if they were learning something they could not use right away.

Flexible groupings can be very beneficial for ESL students when they are in a mixed classroom (a class that consists of both ESL students and students that have English as a primary language). Grouping the ESL students for activities as well as grouping ESL students with other students can be helpful. If the ESL students are grouped together, they can communicate to help each other with their reading difficulties. If an ESL student is paired with an above-average student, he or she could benefit from the positive influence. Both groupings do have drawbacks, however. With the first, the students could lose focus on the activity and communicate mostly in their primary language. With the second, the ESL student could become frustrated and give up, having no one to relate to. Trial and error is about the only way to decipher which is best, so you must evaluate carefully.

Language acquisition

One reason why language acquisition is so complex is that speech sounds are elusive. Even though many people can read fluently, it is likely that many of those people are unable to distinguish each sound within words. Think about it. How many people do you think could accurately separate ten words into separate phonemes? However, this doesn't mean that those who would fail at it wouldn't recognize and understand the words. That is why language acquisition can be difficult. The human brain is designed to understand the meaning of sounds and messages, not each individual part. However, learning through individual sounds is the best way to begin learning language skills.

Language-based learning disabilities

Your goal for teaching a student with a learning problem should be to target the aspects that he or she is missing. For example, if the student can read a passage but not describe the details, then you need to address comprehension. If he or she cannot distinguish the separate sounds within a word, then phonetic skills should be addressed. It is also important that materials used for the individual student relate directly to what is being covered by the rest of the class. The student should be taught how to apply new skills that you have worked on with them to the assignments that you have given to everyone. If necessary, it can be helpful for a specialist to help the student side-by-side in the classroom.

Including cultural diversity

There are four main approaches for including cultural diversity in a learning environment. These are the contributions approach, the additive approach, the transformation approach, and the social action approach. In the contributions approach, the contributions of people of other cultures are added to the instruction. With the additive approach, authors from other cultures are added to the instruction without changing its structure. For example, a book set in Latin America could be added to the classes reading list. In the transformation approach, the content is changed so that the students' viewpoint is the same as that of the targeted group. With the social action approach, students study a problem and are empowered to act on it.

Phonological awareness

Phonological awareness refers to the knowledge that language is made up of smaller parts, such as sounds, syllables, individual words, and sentences. It is a very broad term that encompasses many ideas and areas. By the time a child enters school, they are expected to have basic phonological awareness. While most children have this knowledge, it is up to the teacher to further develop it. For instance, a student might be aware that words are made up of syllables. However, that student might need help with distinguishing syllables within words.

The skills that best separate good readers and poor readers are phonological skills. Poor readers may have good listening comprehension, but they struggle with written language because they lack basic skills, such as phonology. The best early readers are those that are able to distinguish sounds within a written word. At this age, these skills are even more important to reading than intelligence and verbal reasoning. Once students advance to higher grades, such as middle school, phonology is not as important and other skills come into play. It is therefore important for a teacher to place emphasis on phonological skills during the early stages of reading development.

Distinguishing syllables

By the time students enter school, they will most likely have basic phonological awareness. They will possess the knowledge that words are made up of syllables, even if they do not know the term "syllable" or how to distinguish them. A popular method for teaching children to separate words into syllables is the clap method. As you say a word out loud, clap once for each syllable that is pronounced. Then have the child try to do the same. For example, if the word was "happy," the student would need to clap twice—once for the "hap" syllable and once for the "py" syllable.

Phonemic awareness

Phonemic awareness refers to a specific aspect of phonological awareness. It is the knowledge that words are made up of individual sounds and the ability to distinguish those sounds. There are many types of phonemic awareness skills. These include the ability to count the number of phonemes in a word, separate a word into its phonemes, combine phonemes to create a word, and remove or change phonemes to change a word.

Children usually begin school with some type of phonemic awareness. They are then taught how to develop the rest of the skills over the next two years and by the end of first grade, most students should have a sound grasp on the awareness skills previously mentioned.

Language structure

A constant among good readers is their awareness of language structure. Those who learn to read well are aware of this structure at the phonemic level. They understand speech sounds and meaning and how those contribute to the meaning of words and text. They also use this knowledge to recognize patterns and decode unfamiliar words. As this process continues, the readers learn automatic recognition and begin to process words and patterns unconsciously. While some students will enter school with this knowledge or will pick it up quickly, it is up to the teacher to instruct children in an effective order for them to comprehend the entire system.

Phonemic skills

Phonemic awareness skills include the ability to count the phonemes in a word, separating a word into its phonemes, connecting phonemes to form a word, and substituting phonemes to create other words. It is important for a teacher to be able to count the phonemes in a word and relay that information to a student. For example, you should know that the word "rich" is composed of three phonemes—/r/i/ch/. By counting phonemes in a word, you should also be able to separate a word into individual phonemes—another skill. An additional phonemic awareness skill is the ability to blend separate phonemes to create a word. As an example, take the phonemes /b/r/a/n/ch/. When blended, these phonemes create the word "branch."

Finally, there is the ability to delete or substitute phonemes to create a different word. As an example, take the word "mat." By removing the /m/ sound, you are left with the word "at." You can also substitute a sound, such as /ch/ and form the word "chat."

Current research has shown that teaching only one or two methods of phoneme manipulation is much more effective than teaching many types of manipulation. These two types of phoneme manipulation are the blending and segmenting of phonemes in words. Research has also shown that directly relating phoneme instruction to reading and writing is extremely effective. For example, you would first ask a student to blend phonemes orally to make a word. The student then should separate the word into individual phonemes and write them on the board. After writing them, you then have the student read the word out loud. Such an activity combines the two successful types of phoneme manipulation with both reading and writing.

Testing phoneme skills

Students who are in the early stages of their reading education can have phonological awareness but still have trouble separating words into individual phonemes. Asking the student a simple question can be the first step toward recognizing a problem. There are many questions that are associated with phonological awareness. These include giving a student a list of words and asking which words rhyme or which words begin or end with the same sound. However, these questions only deal with one or two phonemes. The best question for students struggling with phoneme separation is to ask them how many sounds they hear in a simple word, such as "sat." If the student cannot hear all three sounds (s/a/t), then he or she probably has trouble with the separation.

Using concrete clues

Using concrete objects or clues is a great way to teach children about the awareness of phonemes. A very common way to do this is to use small blocks with letters on them. Give the child a simple word to spell out using the blocks, and then have him or her place one block on the table at a time for each sound. For example, say you asked a student to spell the word "cat." In order to spell the word correctly using the blocks, the child would have to recognize each individual sound—c, a, and t. By doing this, the student learns both to separate words into phonemes and to combine separate phonemes into common words.

Manipulating phonemes

A good way to teach students to manipulate phonemes is to play a rhyming game. Read the students a story. After you are done reading, choose a word that was used a lot in the story. For an example, use the word "sheep." Write the word "sheep" on a piece of paper and draw a picture of a sheep next to it to give the children a sense of imagery. Next, have the children try and list words that rhyme with "sheep" that you can write below the picture. For example, they might say "jeep, leap, steep," and so on. It is also important that you teach students to find words that begin with the same sounds. Using the previous example, take the word "sheep." List the word on a piece of paper and underline the beginning sound of "sh." Have the students try to think of words that begin with the "sh" sound, such as "show, shock," and so on. As you list each word, underline the "sh" part in each of them.

Reading Development

Reading development stages

The first stage of reading development is the prealphabetic stage. Children do not know that letters represent sounds in written words, but they do understand that written words carry messages. They may have an understanding of some familiar words, but the understanding of most words comes from the context of the words around them. The next stage in reading development is the early alphabetic stage. The approach to reading and spelling changes as students learn a crucial fact. They learn that letters make up the sounds in written words, also known as the alphabetic principle. As their knowledge grows, they begin to read and spell out words by "sounding out" parts of those words. During the later alphabetic reading and writing stage, children slowly begin to recognize all of the sounds within a word and match letters to those sounds. They are able to attempt sounding out complete words, although this can take a considerable amount of time. On the other hand, sight words can be picked up quickly if the students are exposed to them enough.

Showing organization of print

Two important concepts of print that students must learn are how print is organized and that print carries meaning. To show students how print is organized within a book, you can do a simple book "walkthrough." Go through a book with them, from front to back, explaining the purpose of each type of print. You do not have to read any of the material; simply explain what the words are doing there. For example, start by telling the students that the cover of the book shows the title, the author, and so on. The simplest way to show that print carries meaning is to read the children a story. The book should be simple and have pictures that convey the meaning of the story. As you read the book to them, hold up the book so they can see the pictures. The students will begin to tie the information with the pictures and see that the print carries the meaning of the story.

Directionality of print

Before students can begin to read sentences, they must first understand the directionality of print. Prepare a sheet of paper to give to each student. This sheet should have a simple paragraph written on it. To show students the direction in which words flow, draw arrows that move from left to right with the words. At the end of each line, draw an arrow that points to the beginning of the next line. As you read the paragraph aloud, have your fingers follow the arrows, and have the students do the same. As they repeat the process, they will learn that the printed words are read from left to right and top to bottom.

Letters and printed words

One of the concepts of print is knowing the difference between individual printed letters and printed words. As a teacher, you can show this to students as you teach them. As the students learn the letters of the alphabet, they will begin to learn the concept of individual letters. To show them that those letters make up complete words, you can use concrete clues. Use blocks or cards with one letter on each. Show your students how putting these blocks together will form words. Then show them that word as it is printed in a book. With practice, they will become aware of the fact that individual letters are combined to form printed words.

Matching voice with print

To teach students to match voice with print, write a sentence on the blackboard. Read the sentence out loud and point to each individual word as you say it. You can also give each student a copy of the sentence on a sheet of paper. Have them repeat the sentence and point to each word as you do the same thing on the blackboard. In time, they will begin to see that each spoken word matches a printed one. You can also incorporate this into other activities, such as a story time where you read a short story aloud to the class.

Pretend readers

Students who are at an extremely early place in their reading education, such as beginning kindergarten students, have not yet learned how to read but still can have an understanding of certain concepts. If you notice a student that is "pretend reading," or telling a story from a book without actually reading the words, you can determine that this is such a student. Even though the student does not know how to read, he or she has an understanding of some of the concepts of printed material. He or she holds the book correctly and turns the pages properly. The student also has an understanding of the connection between spoken words and words that are written. This is shown by turning the pages of the book as he or she tells the story.

Teaching sight words

Sight words are words that are used with a very high frequency and cannot be decoded using normal phonetic skills. These include words such as "in," "of," and "for." Since it is hard to describe a sight word or give its definition to a student, it is a good idea to teach children these words by using them in meaningful

ways. For example, a student may not understand the definition of "of," but he or she may be able to understand its meaning in the phrase "a box of crayons." To use this method to teach a sight word, try using such a phrase accompanied with a picture. For example, have a picture of a box of crayons with "box of crayons" written below it. The sight word, in this case "of," should be in bold. Using this method will help associate meaning and context with the sight words, making them much easier to recognize and memorize.

Alphabet songs

The alphabet song is used to familiarize children with letters and their names. Each letter is sung, in order, usually to the tune of Twinkle, Twinkle, Little Star. It should be sung every day until all the children know it very well. For variety, you can change the tune to which it is sung. Just make sure that the children do not sing it too fast. You do not want sounds being lumped together. For example, many students will combine "l-m-n-o" into "elemeno" instead of articulating each letter. It may also be helpful to have a large chart of letters so that you can point to each letter as the children sing it.

Shapes of letters

Children not only need to learn how to say and pronounce letters; they also need to be able to recognize their shapes. When beginning to teach letter shapes, it is important that you don't teach capital letters and lowercase letters at the same time. Start with capital letters, since it is usually easier for students to tell them apart. Show them how letters are made up of lines, curves, circles, and dots. You should also show them the similarity between certain letters, such as c and d. Show them how a curved line makes "c" and how adding a straight line makes "d." Try to teach one letter each week and adjust according to how well the children are picking it up. Also, try to avoid teaching similar letters back-to-back, since this can be confusing for students. For example, don't teach "d" one week, followed by "b" the next week.

Matching sounds with letters

To teach students the sounds of letters, write a letter on the board, give its sound, and have the children repeat it. For example, write the letter "m" on the board and say, "This letter has the sound of 'mmmmm.' What is its sound?" Once they grasp one letter, introduce a new letter combined with a letter they are familiar with. For example, if the new letter is "k," write "kmmmkmmk" on the board and have them pronounce the sound of each letter. After the students become familiar with every letter, you can repeat the process with simple words.

Letter sounds within words

To teach students sounds within words, use flashcards that have simple words with pictures of the words on them. Have the children use the picture to identify the sounds/ words on the card. Emphasize the sound you are trying to teach, then blend it with the word. For example, you may hold up a card with the word "bat" on it accompanied with a picture of a baseball bat. Ask them what the object is. When you repeat the word "bat," place an emphasis on the "b" sound. Have the children repeat the word and do the same. You can do the same thing with vowel sounds and ending sounds.

Letter sound games

Teachers often use the game "I Spy" to teach the alphabetic principle and the sounds of letters at the beginning of

words. To play this game, have the children try to identify an object in the room that begins with a certain letter. For example, you can say, "I spy something that begins with the letter 'c.' It keeps you warm." When someone answers correctly (coat), have that student write the letter on the board. Have everyone practice saying the word with emphasis on the given letter (c). Another good way to teach and review letter sounds to students is to play a simple action game. Have the students stand up. As you say each letter, have them perform an action that begins with that letter. For example, if you say the letter "h," they can display their recognition by hopping. This game accomplishes two main things. First, the students must associate the letter to its sound. Next, they must think of a word that uses that sound in order to perform the action.

Invented spellings

During the early alphabetic reading and writing stage, children may begin to spell words based on their current skills. While these spellings most likely will not be correct, they can show signs of phonemic awareness. For example, a student trying to spell "car" and "happy" may write "KR" and "HP." By doing this, the child is showing awareness of the main sounds in each word and associating them with the letters that have the most common sound. However, if a child's spellings show no remote connection to correct sounds, it is a sign that the student does not have a grasp of the alphabetic principle and/or phoneme awareness.

Letter cards

Letter cards are a good way to help students blend consonant and vowel sounds. Begin by placing a card with a consonant on it on the table. Have the student sound out the letter. Place another card on the table, this time a vowel. Have the student sound out this letter. Then place the two cards together and have him or her blend the two sounds. After the student has become proficient at blending the sounds, keep adding letters until a word is formed. By starting with a blend and then proceeding onto a complete word, the children will learn to use the process to sound out words and decode simple words that begin with the same consonant-vowel combinations.

Consonant-vowel combinations

While it is important that students learn to sound out consonant-vowel combinations, this is only half the battle. Students must also learn to recognize common combinations and be able to apply this information to decode unfamiliar words. Flashcards are a good way to help students become familiar with common patterns. Put together a group of cards with common patterns. Go through the deck until every student has become comfortable with each combination and can recognize them. After they can recognize each pattern, give the students practice using them with a decodable text.

Decodable texts

Decodable texts can be a great asset for teaching reading students phonics skills. Including these texts in an early reading program gives students the opportunity to apply phonic concepts and associations that you have already taught them. These students begin to learn phonic skills by associating sounds with letters and then combining those letters to form simple words. Decodable texts consist primarily of simple words to give the children practice with something they are capable of doing, thus giving them more confidence in their reading skills. Doing

so will not only help their current skills, but the added confidence will motivate them to continue learning.

Consonant blends

To help students practice consonant blends and find new words with those patterns, give each student a piece of paper. On the left side, write several words down the column that contain blends. Underline the blend in each word. For example, one word might be "slippery" written on the page as "slippery." Next, have the students use a dictionary to find three words that begin with the same blend and write them on the right side of the page. They should underline the same blend.

The popular children's game of "hangman" can also be used for consonant blends. Choose a word that includes one of the blends that you have covered in class. They must then try to guess the letters of the word before the picture is completely drawn. If needed, you can start out by giving one of letters that is part of the blend. This way, the students will try to think of the blends they know in order to get the other letter.

Consonant digraphs

Unlike consonant blends, consonant digraphs do not keep the sounds of the individual letters. In a consonant blend, such as "cl," both the "c" sound and the "l" sound are kept. They are merely blended together. With consonant digraphs, however, the two letters come together to form one sound that is different. For example, the sound "ch" is a consonant digraph. Neither the original "c" sound nor "h" sound is kept. This can be confusing for students. Up until now, they have been taught to sound out each letter. However, this doesn't work with digraphs. If they begin to sound out the "c" sound, they have already mispronounced the "ch" sound. Therefore, it is up to the teacher to effectively teach the students to automatically recognize them. There are many activities that can be used to help teach students consonant digraphs. The activities used for blends can also be applied to digraphs. Flashcards are a good way to promote automatic recognition. Once students have these memorized, decodable texts can be used to help them use this knowledge to decode unfamiliar words. The dictionary exercise used for blends can also be used. Have the students look up words that contain the same digraphs as the words you give them. The game "hangman" can also be used in the same manner as blends to motivate the students and let them have a little fun while learning.

Word-sort activities

Word-sorting games and activities are a good way for students to enhance their reading skills. A popular word-sorting game involves giving each student his or her own deck of word cards. The students then separate the cards into piles based on similarities of sounds or spelling. For example, you could have them sort the words into two piles—one for short "e" sounds and one for long "e" sounds. Another way would be to have them sort those sounds by spelling. For example, you could have them sort the words with long "e" sounds into piles made up of "ee" spellings and "ea" spellings. It is also extremely important that the words you choose are familiar to the students and can be recognized easily. After reinforcing principles they understand with known words, the students will then find it easier to decode words they don't know.

Word-building activities

Word-building activities are a great way to help students with phonics skills, especially vowel combinations. Give the students a deck of cards that has each consonant written on them. The deck should also include a lot of vowel combinations, such as "ea" and "ou." Have the students experiment with adding consonants before and after the vowel combination cards to create words. This will help them build recognition for commonly used vowel combinations and what words can be made by using them. For added motivation, make a game of it. Have the students write down each word they come up with and see which student can come up with the most words. The student with the most words wins.

R-controlled vowels

The "bossy r" concept is a lesson taught to students to instruct them on the effect the consonant "r" has on vowels. Have six students go to the front of the room. Assign one person as the "r" and assign one vowel to each of the other five. Allow the "bossy r" to "boss" around the other "vowels," telling them to go here or there. Then have the "r" student call on one of the vowel students. That student calls out what sound they make when connected to the letter r. By doing this, students will get a visual for how the letter "r" controls vowels. The game bingo can also help students with r-controlled vowels. When playing bingo, give the students cards that have r-controlled vowel combinations on them, such as "ar." Instead of calling out the combinations, call out complete words that contain them. It is then up to the student to decide which words contain which combinations.

Word-analysis skills

Word-analysis skills are comprised mostly of three basic strategies. These strategies include looking at context clues, word structure clues, and analogy clues. Context clues are clues given by surrounding words and pictures that are used to predict a word's meaning. These are helpful, but usually need to be combined with other clues to decipher the exact meaning of the word. Word structure clues are used to predict a word's meaning from analyzing groups of letters within the word. These groups include prefixes, suffixes, and inflectional endings. Analogy clues are used by comparing the unknown word to words that are known. Usually, these words are very similar in spelling and pronunciation.

Word-attack strategies

Word-attack strategies help students figure out and understand unfamiliar words that they come across while reading. The following strategies are common word-attack strategies:

- Look at the pictures. People, items, or actions that appear in the picture might make sense if that word was placed in the sentence.
- Look for familiar chunks of letters within the word. If you find groups of letters you know, you can combine them to sound out the word.The unknown word to a word that looks the same. Then try using it in the sentence. If the word makes sense, it is likely that the two words are related.
- Read the sentence more than once. By rereading the sentence, you may think of a word that makes sense.
- Continue reading. The word may be used again in another sentence. You can then compare the two sentences to find the word's meaning.

- Use your prior knowledge. Think about what you know about the topic that is being discussed and see if you can find a word that makes sense for the sentence.

Word roots

Word roots are parts of words that hold the meaning of the word. They can appear at the beginning, middle, and end of words. If students become familiar with word roots and their meanings, they will be better equipped to decode unfamiliar words that contain those roots. For example, take the word root "bene," which means "good" or "well." If students are aware of its meaning, they should be able to grasp the meaning of the words that contain the root. Examples are "benefactor" (person who gives money to a good cause), "beneficial" (producing good), and benevolent (showing goodwill). By associating the meaning of "good" to those words, it is much easier to decode their meaning.

Base words and affixes

To be effective at decoding words, students need to be familiar with words that make up the majority of the word (base words) and the groups of letters that are added that affect their meaning (affixes). Once students are introduced to those concepts, an activity can help them use both to create words. Divide the children into groups of three. Assign each group an affix. One member of the group then writes the affix on a large piece of poster board. Have each group come up with base words that they can add to the affix to create new words. Each word should be written on an index card. Then, the students can staple the cards to the poster board to create the new words. Have each group see how many words they can create. The group with the most words wins.

Context clues

Context clues allow students to use surrounding information to figure out the meaning of an unknown word. Three types of context clues are usually used. These are semantic clues, syntactic clues, and picture clues. Semantic clues are meaning clues. Such clues include synonym, antonym, and example clues. These clues use signal words such as "too," "but," and "like" to show a relationship between a known word and the unknown word. Syntactic clues point to the order of the words. In many sentences, the order of the words shows that the missing word should be a verb, noun, and so on. Finally, pictures can helpful. For example, if a picture shows a puppy playing with a ball and the unknown word is a verb, then the word "play" would seem reasonable.

Word structure clues

Word structure clues help students decipher meaning by analyzing groups of letters within the unknown word. There are many groups of letters often used in words that will describe or alter the meaning of the word. Such groups include prefixes, suffixes, and inflections. Prefixes include affixes such as "un-" and "re-." If a word begins with "un-," you know that the word's meaning is most likely the opposite of the base word. For example, a student may know the meaning of "necessary." If that student sees the word "unnecessary," then he or she can conclude that the word means the opposite. The same goes for suffixes and inflections. Suffixes are endings such as "-full" and "-ness." Inflectional endings include the endings "-ing" and "-ed."

Analogy clues

Analogy clues help students decipher an unknown word by comparing it to a word they already know. For example, a student may have seen the word "will" many times, is able to recognize it easily, and knows its meaning. If that student is also familiar with the consonant "f," he or she should have few problems identifying or decoding the word "fill." Teachers can help students develop analogy skills by teaching word families, such as "man, fan, and ran." It is also helpful to use activities that include initial consonant substitution. For example, you could ask the students "What word would I have if I changed the "r" in ran to an "m?"

Word maps

Many words have multiple meanings. When coming across such words, students must recognize that there are different meanings and they must use the context of the surrounding words to decipher the correct meaning. Word maps can help students do this. Have them begin with one word that they draw in the center of the page. They then will branch out from there and find groups of words that include the root word but have different meanings. Not only with this increase their vocabulary, but they will also begin to recognize the root word as a word with multiple meanings. With practice, they can then learn to use surrounding words to find the meaning. Having students use their word maps to form sentences is also beneficial. This will teach them about both the semantic function (the word's meaning) and syntactic function (the word's part of speech) of the words that have multiple meanings.

Homonyms, homophones and homographs

Homonyms refer to the broad category of words that include homophones and

- 22 -

homographs. Homophones are words that sound the same but have different spellings and meanings. These include words such as "hear" and "here" and "their" and "there." Homographs, on the other hand, are spelled exactly the same but have different meanings and can have different pronunciations. For example, take the word "wind." "The wind blows" and you "wind a string." "Wind" is spelled the same in both sentences but has different meanings. You can see how this can be confusing for students learning to read. In order to verify the meaning of such words, students must learn to use the context of the surrounding words. As they begin to learn this, they will probably need to correct themselves when reading a homograph. But, as they progress, they will learn what types of sentences include each word.

Word-study notebooks

Word-study notebooks are a good way to improve vocabulary skills for students who are in the later stages of their reading development, such as middle school students. Have each student keep a separate notebook for this purpose. During independent reading time, or the time they read by themselves, have them write down any word they come across that is unfamiliar to them. They should write down the entire sentence that includes the word, and then make predictions about its meaning based on the context of the surrounding words. They then look up the word in the dictionary and write down its meaning. For further development, have them also write down synonyms and antonyms of the word. Linking words with similar or opposite meanings will help with their conceptual understanding of the unfamiliar words.

Word-study notebooks are a great tool to increase students' vocabulary skills.

However, including an interactive component can even further the effectiveness of the notebooks. Separate the students into pairs and have them share with each other the content of their notebooks. Tell them to work together to write new sentences that include the words written down in their notebooks. Through repeated exposure to these words, the students will improve their understanding and retention of their meaning. Working with a partner will increase motivation and help them communicate their thoughts to another person.

Idioms

An idiom is an expression in which the meaning of the words as a whole is an entirely different meaning than that of the words that are in it. Students usually have fun when learning idioms. They enjoy learning their literal meanings as well as their figurative meanings. A popular way to teach idioms is to discuss both of those meanings. For example, you are teaching students the phrase "hold your horses." First, show its literal meaning. You can do this by holding toy horses in your hand. Next, explain its figurative meaning, which is to be patient or slow down. Introduce another idiom, but this time have the students display both meanings. Have them draw a picture of its literal meaning and then show its figurative meaning by whatever means they can.

Word meanings

Students should learn to use dictionaries to clarify word meanings. However, it is important that they only use them to clarify meaning after they have used other phonetic and word-attack strategies. You do not want students looking up every unknown word in the dictionary. As an exercise, give the students a list of sentences with an underlined word that may have multiple meanings. In order to decipher the meaning, have them look up the word in the dictionary to decipher which meaning is applicable. You should also have them distinguish between the word's denotative and connotative meanings. The <u>denotative meaning</u> refers to the literal meaning of the word, or its dictionary definition. <u>Connotative meanings</u>, on the other hand, refer to the associations or emotional suggestions that are connected to the word. These meanings exist in combination with the denotative meanings for the word. Understanding both types is important when deciphering such words with multiple meanings.

Reading comprehension factors

It has been shown that automatic word recognition has a significant impact on a reader's ability to comprehend the text that he or she is reading. If a student cannot recognize words fast enough, his or her attention will be pulled away from the context and meaning of the sentence. The inability to recognize words also slows down reading speed and may cause the reader to reread the sentence. While initial problems in reading can be overcome by decoding skills, there comes a time when automatic word recognition is mandatory. Reading fluency is also extremely important for reading comprehension. While automatic word recognition is essential for reading fluency, it only goes so far. Reading fluency also includes reading at the proper rate and with proper expression. Many scholars also agree that fluency involves the anticipation of what will come next. Anticipation creates better reaction time and better overall comprehension.

Readers theatre

A readers theatre is an activity that can be held to keep students motivated while they repeat oral readings. The teacher takes a story and adapts it into a play. The script is handed out to each student and everyone learns a part. Each day the students are instructed to practice their parts by reading them aloud with a partner. After several days of practice, they then perform their "play." Repeating oral readings help students develop a faster reading rate and better word recognition. Doing this in the form of a play adds motivation and keeps the practice fun. Students who participate in a readers theatre are not as likely to get bored as students who do standard repeated readings.

Reading fluency sample lesson

A popular lesson for improving reading fluency follows the Orton-Gillingham approach. Select a new text for the class to read. Before they read, introduce words from the text that are new to them. Write these words on the board and have the students break them down by syllables. After the students can read the new words, select a few pages for them skim. They should underline any words that they don't understand or cannot read. Write these down on the board and approach them the same way. During the process, you should encourage the students to use word-attack strategies, such as using sentence context or word analogies, to figure out the meaning of the words. After each student is comfortable with the words, begin oral reading. Have the students take turns reading out loud. Students uncomfortable with reading out loud for fear of embarrassment should not be forced to read. Instead, set aside a time they can read to you privately.

A rereading activity

Repeated reading activities are great way to improve reading fluency and comprehension. They increase word recognition, processing speed, and overall retention. Set aside 15 to 30 minutes each day for repeated reading instruction. Find an isolated, quiet location where you can work one-on-one with a student. Select a passage from 50 to 500 words that fits the student's reading level. The student should be able to achieve 85 to 95 percent word recognition accuracy upon first reading the text. Have the student practice reading the passage until a suitable level of correct words per minute (CWPM) has been achieved. The target level of CWPM varies with grade level. Students should have a CWPM level of 60 by the end of first grade. It increases to 90 for second graders and moves up 10 CWPM for each following grade.

Vocabulary

Numerous studies have shown a direct correlation between vocabulary knowledge and reading comprehension. However, this is not a surprise, as many people make the common sense connection. Messages are made of ideas, and ideas are expressed in words. In order to comprehend ideas, you must know the words that are being used. Another reason for the correlation is how vocabulary knowledge is formed. People learn new words best by associating them with context meaning, not by studying word lists. Since people learn words from context, it makes sense that word knowledge increases the knowledge of the surrounding words and sentences.

Prior knowledge

Prior knowledge and experiences play a big part in reading comprehension. Students use their prior knowledge to draw meaning from information that they read. For example, if a book's topic is about traveling, they may remember travels or vacations that they have taken with their families. They use these memories to attack the similar information and extract meaning. When teaching, it is important to activate a student's prior knowledge to build comprehension. Doing so allows students to make connections while reading. Other students' experiences may also help them make those connections. Teaching with this method will also allow you to identify any knowledge gaps or misconceptions that might hinder a student's comprehension.

Motivation

Motivation plays a key part in reading comprehension. Obviously, if a student is not motivated to read, he or she will not comprehend the text. These students will just "go through the motions" by reading the words but not taking into account their meaning. It is important for teachers to select texts and readings that the students find appealing and allow them to learn at the same time. Motivation also plays an important role in basic reading development. Language acquisition can be very difficult for some, and if those people become discouraged, serious delays in learning can development. In these cases, early intervention is a must to keep students motivated and encouraged to keep learning.

Literal comprehension

Literal comprehension refers to people being able to comprehend parts of reading that are explicitly stated. These parts include identifying main ideas and themes, cause-and-effect relationships, and the sequence of events. For example, a story may include an event where a man opened a door and his dog ran out into the yard. When asked how the dog got out of the room, a student will reply, "because the man opened the door." By identifying a cause-and-effect relationship that is explicitly stated, the student is demonstrating literal comprehension. The student should also be able to describe in what order those things happened—the dog came to the door, the man opened it, and the dog ran out. Once again, the student would be demonstrating literal comprehension by giving the sequence of events.

Inferential comprehension

Inferential comprehension refers to people being able to comprehend reading ideas that are not explicitly stated. This includes making inferences, drawing conclusions, and understanding cause-and-effect relationships that are not explicitly stated. For example, a story may include a statement at the beginning that says a backyard gate is broken. In the middle of the story, a family discovers that their dog has run away. When asked how the dog got out of the yard, a student may reply, "He got out because the gate was broken and wasn't working right." This student is demonstrating inferential comprehension by understanding the cause-and-effect relationship of the broken gate and the dog running away, even though it wasn't stated that way in the text. The student uses his inferences to come to the conclusion that the two events were related.

Evaluative comprehension

Evaluative comprehension refers to the ability of a reader to consciously evaluate what they are reading. This includes the ability to analyze arguments and distinguish fact from opinion. For example, take the following sentences. "My dog's name is Spot. He is one year old and is white with a black spot on his back. He is a very handsome dog and he is very fun to play with." These statements contain both fact and opinion. If a student is asked which statements are facts and replies, "Spot is a white dog that is one year old," that student is distinguishing those facts from the opinions that the dog is handsome and is fun. By doing this, the child is demonstrating evaluative comprehension.

Previewing

Before a student begins reading, it is a good idea for them to preview the text to get a better understanding of what they will read. Have them look at the title. What does the title mean? What do they think the reading will be about? Next, have them look at the structure of the book. How is it broken down? How many chapters are there? Are they organized in a certain way—chronologically or by topic? Then have them analyze what questions they will be able to answer from reading (who, what, where, when, why, and how). By doing these things and previewing the text before reading, there is a much better chance that the students will improve their comprehension.

Setting a purpose

Another comprehension strategy for reading is setting a purpose for reading. This strategy can help students with their comprehension by giving them an idea of what they will be seeking. To set a purpose for their reading, have the students ask questions about the text. Are they being introduced to an entirely new topic? Are they looking for more information about a topic they know a little about already? Are they looking for a central theme, specific details, or both? Do they need to distinguish fact from opinion? These are just a few of the many questions students can ask themselves about their purpose. If students learn to do this regularly, their comprehension skills should improve.

Prior knowledge

Before students begin reading a text, one comprehension strategy that many teachers use is discussing the students' prior knowledge of the topic. By discussing their prior knowledge, students' can use that knowledge to make a personal connection to the text. For example, if a book is about traveling, you would want to discuss the children's thoughts and experiences that are related. What is the farthest they have traveled? Do they go on vacations with their families? What is it like to be at a place they've never been before? By answering these types of questions, students will bring forth relevant information in their mind that will help them prepare for the information they are about to receive.

Predictions

One way to increase students' comprehension is to have them make predictions while reading. This helps in mainly two ways. First, students must comprehend what they have already read in order to make predictions. Second, they will pay close attention after they make predictions to see if they come true. Another comprehension strategy that is used during reading is questioning. While they are reading a text, have students pause and ask themselves questions to monitor their comprehension. The obvious questions that can be used are who, what, where, when, why, and how. This is also a good time for students to revisit the questions they made when they set a purpose for reading before beginning the text.

Strategies after reading

Retelling and summarizing are two good comprehension strategies for students to use after they are done reading. After a student is done reading, have him or her give a brief summary of what happened. Summarizing helps with comprehending main ideas and themes, inferences, and overall understanding of the material. Retelling, on the other hand, helps students comprehend and remember specific details and relationships. Another effective comprehension strategy for students is to have them relate the text to other texts that they have previously read. As shown by the technique of relating the text to personal background knowledge, students comprehend information better when they are able to make connections between what they are reading and what they know. When students are done reading, have them pick out a text that is similar. Have them compare the similarities, such as main ideas, cause-and effect relationships, and inferences. You can also have them compare similarities in language structure, such as word structure, semantic meanings, and so on.

Rereading

Rereading is not only effective for increasing fluency. It is also an effective strategy for increasing comprehension. Rereading texts increases processing speed and factual retention. During rereading, students improve their comprehension because they are able to look at the deeper meanings and ideas of the text. Not only will they have a deeper understanding of the material, but they will also be able to catch specific details that they missed the first time around. Because of the many benefits of rereading, it is a good idea for every teacher to include this as part of their teachings for comprehension strategies.

Independent reading

Independent reading can significantly increase a student's success in reading development. Independent reading refers to reading that students do on their own. It is not assigned, instructed, or checked. Independent reading helps students take meaning from text, improve vocabulary, and increase their background knowledge on a variety of topics. Studies have shown that independently reading as little as ten minutes a day can make a significant difference in reading achievement scores. There are many programs that are used to promote independent reading at different grade levels. One way that has been effective for grade-schoolers is to create library centers within the classroom. These centers have a variety of books placed on shelves that students can read during free time or "check out" and take home. There are also incentive programs. For each book a child independently reads, he or she receives points. After the class reaches a certain amount of points, they are rewarded.

Importance of variety

The material that you select for teaching students about fiction and poetry is very important. It is vital that you select a wide variety of literature to keep students interested and motivated to learn within these genres. Different students respond differently to certain types of literature. Some are interested in mysteries while others are interested in fantasy tales or science fiction. A teacher needs to recognize these differences in order to motivate students properly. Just as with phonetic development, if a student becomes disinterested in a type of literature, he or she may become discouraged and learning development will suffer. Independent reading also plays a key role here. Since you cannot please every student at one time with the area you are studying, you should have books available that students can read independently to continue their reading development.

Characters and settings

Part of students' understanding of fiction comes from the ability to identify the story's elements. An activity can help them identify characters and settings as well as understand the story's sequence of events. After the students are done reading a short story, put six strips of paper on the table. Each strip contains an event from the story. Have them read the sentences and place them in the right sequential order. When they are in order, have them read them again. This time, have them describe the characters that are involved and where these actions take place. By integrating the settings and characters with the sequence of events, the students will learn the concept of the story's elements by how they are used within the context of the text. This is more effective than just trying to describe the elements to the children.

Analyzing problems and solutions

To understand fiction, students also need to identify and understand the plot by realizing what problems and solutions are contained within the story. A way to help students accomplish this is by applying a predicting strategy. Have the students read a story up to the point in which they can identify the plot and/or conflict of the story. At this time, they should pause and identify the problem. Have them analyze it by asking questions and predicting what they think will happen. In what ways do they think the characters will resolve the problem? You can also have them connect the story to themselves. What would they do in that particular situation? By analyzing the problems and predicting solutions, the students will better understand those elements of the story.

Reading aloud comprehension

It is likely that you will come across a kindergarten student that is enthusiastic about listening to a story but still has trouble following the content. The student may show this enthusiasm by engaging in discussion before story, making predictions on what will happen, and showing a personal connection to the characters. After the story is read, however, he or she is confused about what actually happened and in what order. To help this student, you should include a story map or board as part of your instruction. The student obviously has some strength in literary response, and showing a story map to the student during the story will help him or her piece together the sequence of events as the story unfolds.

Fiction

Groups of literary work are generally grouped into two areas—fiction and nonfiction. Fiction describes the large umbrella group of literary work that tells a story using imagined events. Nonfiction, on the other hand, makes factual claims about reality. Fiction includes genres such as fables, folk and fairy tales, fantasy, and mythology. Much fiction is produced for the purpose of educating and is used in school textbooks. It is necessary for teachers to understand the genres of fiction so that they may use them in a constructive way to promote learning development.

Poetry

Poetry is a form of art that uses language in an aesthetic manner. It can be written as independent poems or as part of another work of art, such as plays or music. Poetry is often used to elaborate on words' meanings and to create an emotional response from the reader. Many times, it is written in an ambiguous or ironic manner so that it may be interpreted differently by different people. Basic elements of poetry include meter and rhythm. Meter refers to the pattern made for a certain verse. Rhythm refers to actual sound that is made from the writing. Genres include narrative, epic, dramatic, and lyric poetry. Narrative poetry tells a story. Epic poetry is generally a long version of narrative poetry. Dramatic poetry is dramatic writing that is meant to be spoken. It is usually represented in plays, including Shakespeare. Lyric poetry, on the other hand, does not tell a story. It is mostly used to give the writer's feeling and perceptions.

Mythology, fables, and fantasy

Mythology refers to the body of works described as myths. Myths are stories connected to the spiritual beliefs and traditions of specific cultures. They often use supernatural events and/or characters to explain the universe, existence, and its effect on humanity and its history.

Fables are short stories that use animals, plants, objects, and forces of nature with human qualities to demonstrate a moral lesson. They can be written in prose or verse.

Venn diagrams

Venn diagrams are a great way to organize information based on similarities and differences. They can be especially helpful when trying to teach students about the different types and genres of literature. After explaining each type of literature to the students, draw a Venn diagram on the board. You can compare up to three types of literature at a time. As an example, take two types—

fantasy and fairy tales. Have the students begin by calling out traits of each type. Before you write a trait down on the board, ask them if it is something the two types share and place it accordingly. For example, "happy endings" could go in the fairy tales circle and "magical characters" could be placed in the intersection since both types of literature feature those types of characters. The interaction and visualization should both help students in identifying types of literature.

Webbing

Webbing is a useful method for introducing ideas that have supporting facts. Webbing involves drawing word bubbles for main ideas and then branching off those to create more bubbles that include supporting facts and details. When the drawing is finished, it looks like a giant "web" of information. Webbing has been shown to be quite useful when teaching students about types of literature. Take fables for instance. First, the word "fables" would be written inside a bubble. Next, a line is used connect that bubble to another that says "characters." Branching off that bubble would be bubbles that say "animals," "plants," and so on. Continue drawing until a "web" describing fables is complete. Having students call out traits will help with motivation while the visualization will help with retention and recall. Students also may find it fun to see how big of a "web" they can create with their knowledge.

Identifying themes

The theme of a story is the central idea that brings all the other story elements together. In order for students to identify the theme of a story, they have to know the entire story. Many times in education, theme is confused with topic. The topic of a story can be described by a single word

or small phrase. It simply tells what the story is about. For example, the story is about love. Love cannot be the theme, it is merely the topic. The theme is much more detailed. Once again, in order to identify the theme, students must take into account all the elements of the story. To help students identify the theme, first have them identify the story's elements—plot, setting, characters, conflict, and problem/solution. Then ask the students to tie them together. What is the author trying to tell us by using all of these? Have them share ideas to analyze the information. Once they consider the whole story, they should have little trouble finding the theme.

Visualization

Visualizing characters and events as a story develops helps students comprehend what is going on in the story. Have the students read silently. After an appropriate amount of time, have them pause and describe how they are visualizing the story. In order to do this, they need to draw on their background knowledge and personal experiences to make a connection with the story. Asking them to do this out loud forces them to visualize, something they might not do normally. Engaging the rest of the class in the activity allows the students to draw on the experiences of others as well.

Understanding character motive

Understanding a character's motives can be difficult for students. It can be very helpful if students use their personal experiences to compare and contrast with the characters to understand their motives. An activity can help accomplish this. Have the students draw three columns on a sheet of paper. The headings should be "Things about (character name)," "Things about me," and "Things the same about (character name) and me." Go through the book and show them the pictures, one at a time. Ask them if they do anything that the characters do or if there is something about them that is the same or different from the characters. When they are done, have them sum up the three columns. By comparing and contrasting themselves with the characters, they should be able to better understand their motives.

Benefits of nonfiction

Selecting a variety of nonfiction texts is important when teaching students language. A good variety will expose students to the many dimensions of the human experience, such as philosophy and ethics. Using different nonfiction texts also helps students to learn to adjust their reading skills for different types of texts. This will allow them to use different styles and vocabulary for communicating with different audiences and for different purposes. It is also important for students to learn to use nonfiction texts for research and to support their opinions and conclusion. Choosing a variety of texts will help them accomplish this.

Limitations of textbooks

While content area textbooks can be useful and are used in many classrooms, they also have several disadvantages and limitations. These textbooks are often written above the level of the students that are using them and include technical jargon and vocabulary. Topics covered are usually done so in a very general manner, providing little in-depth insight and knowledge. Content area textbooks also are written with a certain structure that many students struggle to understand, such as descriptive mode with a lack of transitions. Students may also find the subjects boring and of little interest to them. Finally, many of these

texts are outdated and do not describe current events.

Nonfiction trade books

While content area textbooks are used in many classrooms, they have certain limitations and disadvantages when compared to nonfiction trade books. Nonfiction trade books allow teachers to use material that is closer to their students' individual reading levels. These books also contain graphics and illustrations that children find appealing. Nonfiction trade books give in-depth information, not just general information, on a wide variety of topics, people, and places. The content of these books are arranged more logically than content area textbooks and provide more current information. Also, with the increased popularity of their use, these texts are becoming increasingly available through sources such as libraries.

Nonfiction text strategies

An important job for reading teachers is to teach students to adjust their reading strategies for different types of texts. When reading nonfiction texts for information on particular topics, students cannot read in the same manner they use for other types of text. Instead, they need to read selectively and adjust their reading pace based on the content and on the difficulty of the reading. You should teach the students skimming and scanning strategies. Then, if the students come across material that is relevant or difficult to read (such as technical material), they can slow down and read more attentively to increase comprehension and retention.

Graphic organizers

Graphic organizers are sheets prepared by teachers and used by students to conduct research on a certain topic. These sheets of paper are divided into two sides. On the left side, questions about the topic are written down by the student. The right side of the page leaves space for answers to these questions. In order to find the answers, students must research the topic, usually at the library, and take notes as they read. Having the students write the questions themselves forces them to draw upon their current knowledge of the topic. By using a question-and-answer format, the exercise gives a strong purpose to the reading of nonfiction and motivates the students to keep reading.

An important thing for students to learn is how to distinguish between main ideas and supporting details in nonfiction texts. Graphic organizers can help students accomplish this. Go over the text that they will be reading. Next, have them use skimming techniques to locate main ideas. They should use these main ideas to form questions that they write down on the left side of the page. Then have them read through the text to answer the questions. When they are finished, explain to them how the questions they made covered main ideas, while the answers they found describe supporting details. By using the graphic organizers, they should be able to distinguish the difference between the two.

Posing questions

One comprehension strategy for nonfiction texts is posing questions. To help students do this, introduce a topic that the class will be learning about. Divide them into groups so that they can discuss the topic and learn what they each know. Next, have them come up with questions about what they would like to learn about the topic. Then have the class read the nonfiction assignment, keeping in mind their questions so they can read

critically. When they are done, select questions for the class to discuss as a whole. Make sure that students support their answers using specific details from the text. By posing questions and looking for specific details, students will learn strategies for comprehending nonfiction texts.

Skimming nonfiction

Another important comprehension strategy for nonfiction texts that students should learn is skimming. Explain to them that skimming allows them to find the most important information that they are looking for and leave the rest behind. Next, explain your goal for skimming a particular text. Go through your skimming techniques as you look through the material. For example, you may say these lines: "First, I am going to look through the table of contents for any of the key words…Those words are mentioned on these pages, so I'm going to read the entire page…The words are boldface headings here, so I'm going to go through and list details." When you are done, discuss the skimming techniques with the children and have them try to do the same thing.

Connecting with nonfiction

If students are able to connect with a nonfiction text, they will have a better chance of comprehending it. Read the text aloud with the students. When you are done, share one of your own personal experiences that helps you relate with the text. Then use questions to help students make their own connections. Did they ever have a similar experience? Did they connect with any decisions made by the people? Did they learn anything about those people or themselves by reading? Teachings students to relate material to themselves and the people around them will help them understand it and will increase their retention of the material.

Cause-and-effect

One of the main structures within nonfiction texts is cause-and-effect. There are four main cause-and-effect structures that students should know. First, there are basic cause-and-effect relationships, which can be shown with charts. One event specifically causes another event to happen. Second, there are chain-of-event structures. This is when one event causes another event, which causes another, and so on. These can be illustrated by drawing connected boxes in a row with one event in each box. Third, there unrelated events that still have effects on one another. These are best illustrated by using Venn diagrams. Fourth, there are problem/solution structures. This is where one problem poses several solutions, which in turn causes different events to happen.

Compare and contrast

Strategies can be very effective for students studying nonfiction texts. First, you must introduce the concept of the two words. You can do this by introducing two objects, such as apples and oranges. Draw two columns on the board, one for similarities and one for differences. Have the students come up with things for each column as you write them on the board. Explain to them that by listing things that are the same, they are comparing the two objects. By listing things that are different, they are contrasting. Next, introduce clue words for comparing and contrasting that they will find in texts. For example, the clue word "like" is used for similarities. If students come across this word, they should know that two things are being compared. Divide the students into groups to read a nonfiction text. Have them use the clue words to find examples of comparing and contrasting within the reading. They should also write these

down on paper in the same way you did on the board. When they are done, the class should discuss what they found and which clue words they used to find the information.

Using nonfiction texts

There are a variety of reasons why students need to learn to use nonfiction texts. One of these reasons is to support their opinions and/or conclusions. After covering a topic, have the students give their opinions on the matter. When they are done, group the students that share the same opinion. Then, give them the assignment of looking through nonfiction texts to find facts that support their opinion. You can even make a game of it. For every fact they find that supports their particular opinion, that group gets one point. If a group finds a fact that argues another fact found by another group, those two are cancelled out. If a group finds two facts that argue one fact, then that group gets one point and so on. The group with the most points wins.

Writing as developmental process

Learning to write is a developmental process. Teachers who recognize writing as a developmental process give students more responsibility for their own learning. Students choose their own topics and use their experiences and observations to write about them. Teachers who recognize writing as a process are also aware of the recursive nature of writing. There are certain steps that students go through during the process—prewriting, writing, revising, editing, and publishing. Some students may go through these stages in order, while other may repeat certain steps before completion. For these reasons, teacher must evaluate the entire process, not just the finished result. Proper assessment should be done during each stage in the writing process so that feedback can be the most effective.

Writing to describe

Writing to describe is an interesting type of writing that is not used very often. It is used solely to describe and does not take the form of other writing purposes. When writing to describe, it is best to think of yourself as a human camera. Your job is to take a snapshot of what you are describing. This keeps you from evolving your writing into a story. When writing, you want to create vivid imagery. You don't want to simply tell the audience, you want to show them. Create good mental pictures by using descriptive words. Don't use too many, however. Instead, use precise words. By choosing your words carefully, you will describe better and create better mental images.

Writing to inform

When you are writing for the purpose of informing, you are trying to tell the audience something they need, want, or would like to know. You must use this knowledge to write in a style that is appropriate for your target audience. Information must be clear, trustworthy, and well-supported. It should answer the five Ws—who, what, where, when, and why—as well as how. The most important part of writing to inform is including facts. Facts should be balanced and unbiased. You should not allow yourself to show your opinion on the matter. In order to have unbiased information, you should use multiple sources that reflect different viewpoints. Finally, you need to write in a confident, but honest, tone.

Writing to persuade

Writing for the purpose of persuading is similar to writing for the purpose of arguing, although they are different.

When writing to persuade, you have the single purpose of trying to change the minds of your audience. Writing to argue, on the other hand, involves giving a convincing argument that tries to counter other views. While arguments tend to rely on using reason alone, persuasive writing also relies on creating an emotional response. When writing to persuade, your first goal is to catch the audience's attention. You then give your opinion and back it up using logical and emotional arguments. Make a strong point, but don't make it seem like you are pleading. Never state the obvious, and don't try to attack opposing arguments by calling them foolish.

Writing to entertain

Writing for the purpose of entertaining usually involves writing a story. The most important part of this type of writing is developing a main idea or message. The entire story will revolve around this idea. There are four keys to writing a successful story. First is planning. You must think about who will be in it, where it will take place, what will happen, and why this will interest the audience. Second, don't write anything that doesn't need to be written. Avoid adding anything that doesn't contribute to the relevance of the story. Third, create a mood and setting that will help your audience feel like they are there. Fourth, don't describe for the sake of describing. Make your descriptions mean something and add to the story. If they don't, then leave them out.

Replicating patterns

One way that has been shown effective for improving writing skills is having students replicate patterns found in literature. Students see the effective writing and try to apply it to their own writing. One type of source that is used with this approach is the pattern book. Pattern books use simple, repetitive language and allow children to anticipate what comes next. Topics and illustrations are usually something that the children can relate to. For example, one page may have a picture of a cat with a sentence below it. The next page has a similar picture with a sentence that contains blanks. The children use the pattern of the language from the previous page to fill in the blanks and write the sentence.

Readers' theatre and writing

While a readers theatre focuses mostly on improving students' reading skills through repeated oral readings, it can also be a helpful tool for teaching creative writing skills. Separate the children into small groups and have them write their own story. Each student should be given an equal part in both the writing and performing aspects of the project. If they are having trouble coming up with ideas, they may rewrite a current story or adapt it to their own lives. Writing these stories is a good way to teach students creative writing while keeping them entertained. It helps them make a connection between reading and writing, and working their peers furthers this development.

Language experience approach

The language experience approach is an approach to writing that is based on activities made from the personal experiences of the students. This ties into the idea that writing is a developmental process. With the language experience approach, activities may include students choosing their own topics and writing about them using their own ideas and personal experiences. There are many advantages to the language experience approach. It brings together reading, writing, and language. It develops creativity and helps students understand that what they know can be written down. It also is centered around the learners and shows them how their thoughts and ideas matter.

Writing and Research

Prewriting

Prewriting is the first stage of writing. This is the stage where a writer brainstorms to gather ideas and get them down on paper. There are many ways to help students get ideas. These include looking through periodicals, drawing from personal experiences, brainstorming through discussion, and taking personal interest inventories. The main point of prewriting is getting as many ideas as possible. Even though they will not use all of them, they need to have a wide selection of ideas to choose from. As they come up with ideas, the next step is to get them down on paper. Graphic organizers, lists, and free writing are great ways to help students get their ideas written down.

Writing

The writing, or drafting, stage is the second stage in the writing process. This is when the writer uses ideas gathered from the prewriting stage to create a rough draft. When helping students in this stage, there are four main points to remember. First, students need to be selective when choosing from their prewriting ideas. They don't have to include everything. Have them pick their best ideas. Make sure, however, that they are related to each other and the topic. Second, they should write as much as they can. Once they start writing, they shouldn't stop. Editing comes later. Just let the ideas flow. Third, do not give them a required length until they are done writing. They should just keep writing until they feel that their ideas have been covered. Fourth, if they then come up short, have them go back to their

prewriting ideas to select more to write about.

Revising

The third stage of the writing process is the revising stage. This is where students attempt to look at their writing from a different point of view to see how they can make it better. The goal of revising is to make writing clearer, more interesting, more informative, and more convincing. A popular method for revising is the A.R.M.S. method. This stands for adding (What else do they need to know?), removing (What information is unnecessary?), moving around (Is the information in a logical order?), and substituting (Would different wording or phrasing make things clearer?). To help students see their writing from a different point of view, have students read each others work and make suggestions. No names should be on the papers. Small groups are good for this and allow each student to get three to five different viewpoints about their work.

Editing

The editing stage is the fourth stage of the writing process. During this stage, a writer goes over the writing with a "fine-toothed comb." During editing, students check for things such as spelling, grammar, punctuation, capitalization, and correct verb usage. Both self-editing and peer editing can be helpful during this stage. One particularly useful albeit strange method is to have the students read their writing backwards. They should read the last sentence first, then the next to last sentence, and so on. This increases focus and forces the student to look at each sentence by itself. This especially helps with things such as grammar, punctuation, and spelling. Having fellow students look over each others work is also beneficial. This can be done in the same manner as group revisions made during the revising stage.

Publishing

The publishing stage is the final stage of the writing process. During this stage, the final copy of the writing is made to be handed in. Different teachers will have different requirements for the final copy. However, the following are the most common: Words are printed in blue or black pen. The student's name, class, and date are placed at the top, right-hand corner. Words are printed neatly and paragraphs are either single- or double-spaced, depending on whether the teacher needs room for corrections. Words are written on only one side of the paper and pages are numbered. Many teachers will also have students hand in rough drafts and any prewriting works at this time as well. This allows them to monitor the development of the writing during the entire writing process.

Central idea and details

Communicating the central idea is the most important part of good writing. You need to make sure that the message that is intended for the audience is actually being expressed. By focusing on the central idea, you show an understanding of that idea and that you are able to communicate it to the audience. Always keep in mind the question you are answering. Good writers convey their main ideas through support and elaboration of details. Supporting details must be given in a clear and relevant manner. Using concrete details strengthens the writing and the response of the reader. Determining whether details are supportive is accomplished through the concepts of relatedness and sufficiency. Relatedness refers to the direct correlation between the details and the main idea. Sufficiency refers to the weight and emphasis that is placed upon the details. For example, poor sufficiency comes from undeveloped details or redundancy.

Logical structure

Creating logical structure, or good organization, is essential for effective writing. This is shown by providing a logical flow of information and creating an effective beginning, middle, and end of the composition. Good beginnings are important because they draw in the attention of the reader. Poor beginnings can discourage readers from continuing further. The middle of the composition depends on the genre. Usually one of five organizational structures is used. These are sequences, descriptions, cause and effect, compare and contrast, and problem and solution. Endings can be just as important as beginnings. Good endings wrap up the composition and make the audience remember the main points of the presentation. Poor endings can leave the audience feeling unimpressed and can undo any effective writing up to that point. Using coherent transition words also helps with structure and the flow of the writing. Transitions allow the reader to move seamlessly from one detail to another.

Unity

Unity is an important aspect for effective composing. The concept of unity can be applied to both paragraphs and an entire composition. For simplicity sake, we will look at paragraph unity. Paragraph unity means that one paragraph only discusses one topic. This means that all the sentences—topic, supporting, detail, and concluding—tell the reader about one thing. If a paragraph contains a sentence that does not directly relate to the main idea, then it is said that the paragraph lacks unity.

Precise vocabulary

One of the things that can ruin effective writing is trying to be too descriptive. The writer tries to describe every noun by using adjectives and adverbs. Overuse of adjectives and adverbs can actually take away from the description. Now, adjectives and adverbs have their place and should be used. However, they should undertake a secondary role in that they can be used to help out words that otherwise aren't very descriptive. More importantly, precise words should be used whenever possible. Instead of using more words to describe a noun, replace the noun with one that is more descriptive. For example, take the sentence, "She walked in a carefree way down the street." Precise vocabulary should be used instead—"She strolled down the street." This sentence is just as descriptive and uses more succinct words.

Voice and tone

Two important aspects of writing are voice and tone. Voice and tone show your attitude about the subject you are writing about. Voice refers to who the audience hears while reading, while tone refers to the overall expression of the writer's attitude. Basically, voice is the person saying it and tone is the way they say it. Voice can range from academic to personal to detached. Academic voice is more formal and informative. Personal voice connects you with the reader. Basically, they hear your distinct attitude. Detached voice is ineffective in writing and should not be used. When a detached voice is used, the reader feels no connection to the author or the information. Tone is usually informative or affective. Informative tone simply gives the audience information while affective tone tries to persuade the audience in some way.

Sentence variety

Sentence variety is important in written expression because it keeps writing from becoming boring and repetitive. There are two main ways to increase sentence variety. These are varying the length of sentences and varying sentence openings. By varying the lengths of sentences, you vary the writing's rhythm. Good writing always contains a mixture of long and short sentences. Long sentences are good for giving a lot of information. Short sentences are useful for placing emphasis on main points. You can also obtain sentence variety by varying the beginning of sentences. Too many sentences begin with the common words "I," "The," "This," or "It." Changing sentence openings not only changes sentence structure, but it also allows for you to vary the amount of emphasis used on a particular sentence.

Written retelling

Just as oral retelling and summarizing can improve a student's reading comprehension, written retelling and summarizing can accomplish the same thing. Writing activities are a good way to reinforce reading comprehension strategies. After a student is done reading, have them retell what they just read by writing it down. By retelling, students must recall specific details and the sequence of events from the text. You can also have them write a written summary about what they just read. In order to do this, they will have to remember main ideas and relationships from the text, such as cause-and-effect relationships or any problems that were resolved. By writing it down, students focus on the words they are using and can establish a connection between what they are thinking and what they are writing.

Inferential comprehension

Writing is one tool that reading specialists can use to develop inferential comprehension. Inferential comprehension refers to how a student interprets a story based on information that is not explicitly stated in the text. The student draws his or her own conclusions, or infers, by "reading between the lines." For example, a student might take implied meanings from the story and use their prior knowledge about the topic to make a prediction about the outcome. To help develop inferential comprehension, a reading specialist could have students read part of a story. The students are then separated into pairs and told to write their own endings for the reading. After they are done, they read the actual ending and compare it to the endings they wrote. By doing this, they can see how accurately they read between the lines. This strengthens the students' ability to make inferences while reading.

Conclusions from student writing

A student who writes "Are u hp to c me?" is trying to write "Are you happy to see me?" The conclusion you should make about this child's writing is that the student has knowledge of basic phonetic principles but at times will substitute letter names for letter sounds when trying to spell. The student shows that he or she can connect certain sounds to the appropriate letters, such as the beginning letters in "happy" and "me." However, he or she uses the letters "u" and "c" in place of the words "you" and "see." The patterns this child demonstrates are completely normal and are present in the early phonetic stage of spelling development.

Language acquisition and spelling

Spelling development (the orthographic stage) is closely connected to language acquisition and builds off the foundation made by the stages of acquisition. The following illustration should be helpful to understand the correlation.

Prealphabetic   Early alphabetic Later alphabetic Orthographic

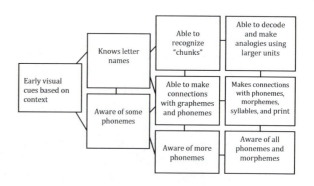

Word sorts

Introducing word sorts is a good way to introduce words that have similar sounds. By studying and analyzing these words, students can learn similarities in spelling and apply them to their writing. A popular way to introduce word sorts is by using word walls. Word walls sort words by sound and are grouped in vertical columns along the walls of the classroom. There are many different ways to sort words. These include sorting by words that start the same, words that end the same, rhyming words, words with the same number of syllables, words that are the same part of speech, words with affixes, synonyms, antonyms, and compound words. Word families are similar to word sorts but are more specific. Word families contain words that are made from the same groups of letters and have similar sound. Words are usually grouped by ending sounds. For example, common groupings include "-all" (ball, call, fall) and "-ate" (ate, fate, crate).

Identifying complete sentences

Once students understand the concept of complete sentences and that each sentence must include a subject and a predicate, activities can be used to reinforce that knowledge. Have each student make two cards—one that says "sentence" and one that says "not a sentence." Read aloud a phrase or sentence and have students raise the appropriate card. This activity is also good for assessing which sentences the majority of the class understands and which they need help with. Another helpful activity involves writing incomplete sentences and complete sentences on different sentence strips. Hand out the strips to the class. Put two columns on the board—one for fragments and one for sentences. Have each student come to the front and put their strip in the appropriate column. When all the strips have been placed, go over them with the class. Have the class complete any sentences that need it.

Word agreement

A good way to teach students pronoun-antecedent agreements is through visual imagery. This particular activity uses Lego blocks to accomplish this. Divide students into groups of two or three. Each group will look at sentences you place on the board and determine the antecedent and the pronoun. Students will have a combination of small Legos and large Legos. The small blocks represent singular pronouns and antecedents while the large blocks represent plural pronouns and antecedents. When students identify the antecedent and the pronoun, they hold up the appropriate block. If the blocks fit together, the students are correct. If they don't, then they have a visualization of the problem and can fix it. This activity will also work with subject/verb agreement. For this,

use a certain color for subjects and another color for verbs. The size indicates whether the subject or the predicate is singular or plural.

Punctuation

Two important areas in punctuation are the use of apostrophes and the use of commas. Many students struggle with the use of apostrophes. This is mainly because apostrophes are used for both contractions and to show possession. An effective lesson on apostrophes includes teaching students to understand the difference in the two uses. Using an overhead, display a passage of text that the students have already read. Have them identify each word that contains an apostrophe. Underline each of those words, and discuss whether each word is a contraction or possessive. As a group, put each word into the appropriate category on the board. A good exercise for commas is to write a passage on the board, excluding the commas. Have students take turns coming up to place commas in the appropriate place. If a student is having trouble, have them read the sentence out loud. As they read, they should place commas where they naturally pause while speaking.

Capitalization

An important lesson for students to learn is which nouns are proper nouns and that proper nouns need to be capitalized. One common way to do this is through name association. Most students understand that names of people are capitalized. Use this knowledge to associate it with names of other words. For example, "boy" would not be capitalized, but the name of a boy, such as "Steve," would be capitalized because it is a name. The word "month" is not capitalized, but "March" is because it is the "name" of a month. This technique can be used with most proper nouns and is usually grasped by students with ease. Another way that is used to help students identify proper nouns is to have them look through magazines and cut out pictures. They then stick them on a poster with two columns—one for proper nouns and one for common nouns.

Research

The same techniques that are used for comprehending nonfiction can also be used when students are conducting research. These include questioning, previewing, and scanning. Before beginning research, students should ask themselves what questions they would like answered. These can include general ideas as well as specific details. Next, they should preview the text they will be reading. What does the title mean? What information do they expect to find? How is the text organized? Finally, using skimming techniques will allow them locate the most pertinent information. Skimming also allows them to adjust their reading pace based on the subject matter. By using these comprehension strategies, students will conduct research more effectively and will have a better chance of comprehending what they find.

Organizing information

Students should learn that writing techniques can be applied to research in order to organize information and record it effectively. Two important writing techniques that students should learn are outlining and note taking. Outlining is a good way to organize information when doing research. Once they can create an outline, they should be shown how to take good notes. Show them how to expand on the outline to produce relevant information in an organized manner.

Graphic organizers are also a great way to put together ideas and communicate

them. Have the students use the information they have written in their organizers to compose a paper on the topic. Each question should serve as one paragraph. Show them how they can convert each question into the topic sentence for each paragraph, and then use the answers to support the main idea and complete the paragraph. Using this format will help them organize the information into paragraphs with good structure and effectively communicate what they have learned through their research.

Text organizers

Two text organizers that are helpful for finding and categorizing information are an index and a table of contents. Indexes allow students to find specific information that they are seeking. While a table of context can give them a general idea of where information might be, an index can give specific page numbers. Also, indexes are helpful when looking for information that is in multiple chapters. This way, students will not have to look through each chapter that might contain what they are seeking.

While a table of contents can help students find information, it can also be used to categorize information. For example, a student may need to find certain information from different areas. After finding it, however, he or she still needs to categorize it in the proper areas. Looking at the table of contents can help with this. Since the table of contents is organized by chapter and by groups of information, using it will allow the student to find where the information fits.

Dictionaries and thesauruses

A simple activity can help students learn to use the dictionary and the thesaurus effectively. Give students a list of words for them to look up. These words should be new words. However, they can be conceptually related to words they have already studied so that they can make a connection to the new words. Have each student look up the words in the dictionary. When they are done, have them read aloud each word's meaning, spelling, and pronunciation. You can also have them note how dictionaries show each word's syllable structure. Next, tie this exercise to the thesaurus. Have the students look up the same words in the thesaurus and read aloud any synonyms and antonyms they find. If the words they look up are conceptually related to previously learned words, they may find that the words they find in the thesaurus are words that they already know. This will help students with learning the concept of the thesaurus.

Encyclopedias

Young students are fascinated with the world around them and enjoy learning about it. By using encyclopedias, students are encouraged to learn more about a topic that interests them, such as animals. In fact, studies have shown that when given a choice, young children will choose nonfiction texts over fictional texts half the time. When introducing encyclopedias to a young grade, research should be done as a class. Have the class vote on an animal they wish to research. Have them make up questions that they would like answered when they do their research. Then, allow them to look through the encyclopedia to try and find the answers. Have the students record their findings in a graphic organizer so they can see the information in a clear, organized manner. When they are done, discuss the findings as a class and have them share their thoughts on what they learned by using the encyclopedia. You can also have them contrast that information with what they would have learned if they used a different type of text.

Glossaries

Glossaries are an important tool and students need to learn to use them when they are reading texts. Begin by introducing texts that include glossaries. Show the students how words that are described within the text can be looked up in the back of the book. You should also note the difference between a glossary and an index. Indexes only give what page the information is on, whereas glossaries give the definition of the word. As an activity, have students read a section of the text and write down any words they are not familiar with. Then have them look these words up in the glossary and write down their meanings. Afterward, have the students discuss what they learned about glossaries. Did they help with understanding the meaning of the unfamiliar words? Were there any words that weren't in the glossary? If there were, why do they think they were missing?

Multimedia presentations

Multimedia presentations can be overwhelming for many students. The amount of choices available and tasks that need to be accomplished can be very distracting. After the students have completed their research and are ready to begin on the actual presentation, their first step should be to make a storyboard or plan an outline. Making a storyboard will help them focus their thoughts and break down the presentation into easy, manageable steps. If the preparation will take several days, have them cover only part of the outline each day. Breaking the project down into easier steps increases the chance that the information will flow freely and logically.

Evaluating media resources

Evaluating resources that you plan to use is important for any teacher. This is especially true for media resources, such as the Internet. With the popularity of the use of Internet resources, you need to be able to distinguish between good and bad sites and sources. After all, anyone can put information on the Internet. Here are a few tips for evaluating such sources:

- Check for accuracy. Does the information given check out with other sources? Does the source use editors or fact checkers to ensure accuracy?
- The source needs to be objective. There should be little bias with the exception of analysis of any facts that are given. Find out who publishes the material. Do they have any specific intentions?
- The information needs to be timely. Media sources, especially the Internet, should include when the information was last updated. Also, when using Internet sources, check to see if there is update information specific to that page, not just the entire site.
- Finally, research the authors. Do they seem credible? Are they considered experts on the topic?

Specialized Knowledge and Leadership Skills

Signs of disability

Different students develop skills at different rates. They also differ in which skills they excel at and which skills they struggle with. However, it is important to be aware of signs at each stage that could point to learning difficulties or a language-based learning disorder. Signs during early stages include difficulty in processing sounds, difficulty with comprehension, and difficulty finding the right words to express ideas. Signs in later stages of development include delays in vocabulary development, problems with understanding grammar, and difficulty with remembering sequences. If these symptoms seem either abundant or persistent, it is a good idea to assess the student for a language-based learning disability. If the student is just experiencing difficulties in reading, then tailored instruction should be given.

Key facts

Learning disabilities are neurological disorders. Children with learning disabilities may appear as smart as other children, but they have trouble learning from conventional methods and along average timelines. These disabilities cannot be "fixed." They are lifelong issues that must be addressed at each level of language acquisition. According to the National Institute of Health, one in seven Americans has some type of learning disability. Learning disabilities that are associated with reading and language skills are the most common. These include dyslexia, dysgraphia, auditory and visual processing disorders, and nonverbal learning disabilities. While attention disorders, such as Attention Deficit/Hyperactivity Disorder, are not the same, they often occur at the same time. Therefore, reading specialists should also be aware of such disorders.

Dyslexia

Dyslexia is a language-based disability in which a student has trouble understanding written words. It interferes with everyday activities that require reading and disables students enough that they fall below requirements expected of their age and level of education. A dyslexia diagnosis also requires that the condition is not due solely to a sensory disorder, such as a vision problem. Students with dyslexia may have good oral language skills, but their written skills suffer. Despite how it is commonly portrayed, dyslexic individuals do not see words backwards or upside down. However, misspelling of words is very common. For instance, a student may leave out all vowels when trying to spell a word. Dyslexics also have excellent long-term memories. Because of this, young students tend to memorize strains words as they learn to read. However, they struggle when trying to read words individually.

Dysgraphia

Dysgraphia is a writing disability in which students find it difficult to form letters or write within a defined space, regardless of their ability to read. Three types of dysgraphia exist—dyslexic, motor, and spatial. With dyslexic dysgraphia, students can usually copy written work well, but spontaneous written works are illegible. Spelling also suffers. Motor dysgraphia involves deficient fine motor skills. These students may be very intelligent, but they struggle with coordination and can find fine motor skills, such as tying shoes, difficult. Written works are almost always illegible. However, spelling is not affected. Students with spatial dysgraphia cannot understand space as it applies to writing. Dysgraphia can occur in one, two, or all three of these forms. Treatment includes treating impaired motor skills and/or impaired memory and neurological problems, depending on which type of dysgraphia is diagnosed.

Auditory and processing disorders

Auditory and visual processing disorders are disabilities in which students have difficulty understanding language despite normal hearing and vision. Students with auditory processing disorders have trouble paying attention to and remembering instruction given orally. They have poor listening skills and take more time to process information. These students should be placed with teachers who have a clear and organized speaking style, explain well, and encourage questions. This way, students do not have to decode complex verbiage. Students with visual processing disorders have trouble with things such as visual memory and visual sequencing. These students should be taught orally whenever possible. When given written instruction or tests, clear distinction between ideas or questions must be given. Color-coding usually works well for these areas.

Nonverbal learning disabilities

Nonverbal learning disabilities can be difficult to recognize. Students with this disorder are unable to recognize and translate nonverbal cues, like facial expressions or voice tone, into meaningful information. Such students are sometimes mislabeled as emotionally disturbed because of their responses to

such cues. Dysfunction occurs in four main categories. These are motor (lack of coordination), visual-spatial organization (difficulty with spatial relations), social (problems with nonverbal communication), and sensory (problems associated with any of the five senses). Intervention during times when these problems occur is necessary, and some instruction can overcome these deficits. However, most success comes when students with nonverbal learning disabilities are taught to rely on their verbal strengths to overcome their weaknesses.

ADHD

Attention Deficit/Hyperactivity Disorder, also known as ADHD, is a psychiatric condition that appears in some children, usually during their preschool and early school years. Around 5 percent of children have ADHD, which means in a class of 20, it is likely that at least one student has the disorder. Children with ADHD have a hard time controlling their behavior and paying attention. Since these are characteristics of most children, albeit it to a smaller extent, it is difficult to diagnose and a thorough examination must be done by a qualified professional. ADHD is usually controlled through medication, such as the stimulant Ritalin. However, behavior therapy can also be effective. The best treatment depends on each individual.

High ability students

High ability students have needs that differ from other students. These needs are usually categorized in two areas— learning environment and curriculum. It has been shown that high ability students thrive in a learning environment that is made up of students with the same abilities. Another need for these students is to have teachers that are trained to educate gifted students. Many programs have been set up to satisfy these two needs, with mixed results.

Curriculum needs are also very important. Gifted children tend to be educated at a pace that is too slow. Many of these students either already know the material or they pick it up quickly. They are then left with "leftover" time. Instead of wasting this time, students should have opportunities to learn at a higher level. If curriculum needs are not met, these children will suffer from boredom and may act out or remove themselves from the learning process.

Three common ways of adapting learning environments for high ability students are pull-out programs, grouping, and grade-skipping. Pull-out programs take high-achieving students out of their regular class a few times each week and group them with students of the same ability. The advantage to this is that the students get to work with other high ability students and at a higher level. Disadvantages include the fact that it only occurs a few times a week, so there is little continuity. It also causes students to be labeled.

Grouping students with high abilities allows them to challenge each other on a high level. It also allows teachers to better meet the needs of each student. Drawbacks to grouping are minimal. However, grouping can lead to students being labeled as well.

Grade skipping allows students to enter an environment that challenges them. However, social and emotional problems may result if they feel out of place with their peers.

While learning environments have a great impact on the success of high ability students, the type of curriculum also play a significant role. Two types of curriculum

are generally used. One type is to have a large amount of standards placed within each grade level, covering much of the same topics in each grade. The advantage in doing this is that high ability students can assist their classmates and serve as role models. The downside is that these students can become bored as they see the same material at each level. They also see little relevance in the material since most topics are not discussed in-depth.

The second way to address curriculum is to have few standards with in-depth study of each. Different topics are studied at each grade level, and curriculum can be differentiated based on students' abilities. The advantage to this is that students can work at their own level, and high ability students find studies engaging since topics go much more in-depth. Disadvantages are few as long as it is handled correctly.

Psychology and literacy development

One theory of developmental psychology holds that there are three stages of learning. These are acclimation (when a student enters a new domain), competence, and expertise. As a student goes through these stages, knowledge, interest, and processing skills determine literary development. For example, when students enter acclimation, their interest can be either individual or motivated by a teacher. As they learn and enter competence, their interest becomes solely individual and this carries them to expertise. Processing skills also follow these three stages. For example, surface strategies for processing, such as taking meaning from text, occur during the earliest stage. As a student continues toward competence and expertise, deeper strategies emerge and students turn to critical and analytical processing skills.

Cultural backgrounds

Different cultures have different approaches for coding language sounds into symbols. Reading specialists must be aware of this fact in order to properly assess and instruct students from various cultural backgrounds. These systems are either logographic or phonographic. Logographic systems are based on meaningful units. For example, Chinese uses script that is based on words, and Hebrew and Arabic have consonant alphabets with no vowels. Phonographic systems are based on phonemes. Examples are English and most other European languages. These languages have phonetic alphabets that consist of both consonants and vowels. Orthographic systems, or spelling systems, are also influential. For example, Spanish and Finnish have shallow orthographies. They have a consistent relationship between their sounds and their graphemes. English, on the other hand, has a much deeper orthography, leading to more difficult reading.

Comprehension requires that readers make mental models of the content they are reading. To do this, they must recognize the organizational structure of the text. Different cultures have different organizational formats. Therefore, readers from other cultures break down texts differently. For example, English texts are straightforward. One point follows another in a direct manner. Arabic and Hebrew, on the other hand, have parallel structure and rely on coordinate construction. Asian texts are indirect, and the romantic languages often include extra material. These differences cause English speakers problems because of the change in structure. The same is true for second language readers trying to learn English. Therefore, it is important that teachers realize these differences in order to instruct students from other cultures in an effective way.

Assessment and motivation

How teachers assess their students has a large impact on what is learned and how students view the meaning of instruction. While assessments need to be authentic and should be revised to make improvement, teachers also need to understand how evaluations affect their students. How do the students react to assessments that are problem-based? Do they react differently if questions are multiple choice? How does evaluation affect their efforts? By answering these questions, teachers will be able to realize that there is a correlation between assessment and student motivation and learning.

Testing principles

The principles of good educational measurement and evaluation are often debated, but most educators agree on certain basic concepts:

- Good assessment improves instruction. While assessment helps students' motivation and learning, it also helps the teacher. Teachers can use evaluations as a way to see what is working and what methods students respond to.
- Good assessment is fair. Teachers should show no bias when evaluating and students should have an opportunity to learn the material that is being assessed.
- Good assessment uses many methods. There is no one test that can accurately evaluate students. Teachers need to use a variety of methods and evaluations to test each aspect of a student's education.
- Good assessment is efficient. While many methods need to be used when evaluating students,

proper discretion also needs to be used. Schools have limited resources and teachers have limited time with their students. A teacher must find the proper combination of both methods and resources to evaluate effectively.

Predictors of achievement

Current research has shown that many skills exhibited by students beginning kindergarten can be used as predictors for their reading achievement at the end of that school year. These include recognition of sight words, written and oral comprehension, a strong vocabulary, and listening and speaking skills. However, this research has shown that the best predictors at this level for reading achievement are letter identification and phonemic awareness. Of all the reading skills, these are the most critical. Students who show phonemic awareness and letter-identification skills at the beginning of kindergarten are the most likely to show great progress in their reading development by the end of kindergarten and even first grade.

Peer Tutoring

An effective teaching tool that has surfaced as a result of current research is Classwide Peer Tutoring. Classwide Peer Tutoring allows each student to get one-on-one help and adequate time to learn. With this method, each student in the class is paired with another. The teacher prepares lessons in which one student can teach another. That student teaches the material, asks questions, and tells the other if his or her answers are correct. Researchers have shown this to be effective for both large and small class sizes, and for all different types of students. It is also effective with students who have problems paying attention,

problems with learning, and problems with behavior.

Mission statements

A mission statement gives the fundamental goals and areas of needed improvement for a reading program. It also serves to motivate members of the local community to get involved in achieving those goals. Before creating a mission statement, a reading specialist needs to contact people involved to find out their educational beliefs, goals, and expectations. Sometimes, literacy teams are formed to do this. These teams survey the thoughts of local members of the community, parents, school officials, and the teachers. The literacy team then uses that information to create a mission statement that reflects the views of those surveyed. It is also vital that state and district standards are taken into account when making the statement and trying to implement changes in the reading program.

Reading groups

When beginning a reading program, you must decide how you want to set up the reading groups. Reading groups are set up based on assessment. One way is to wait to set up groups for the first two weeks of school. During this time, introduce the students to the reading centers, structure of the program, materials and so on. Once they can work independently, begin assessing students one at a time. Once you are done with every assessment, you can group the students and create lessons for each group's needs.

Another way is to groups students based on assessments made at the end of the previous school year. With this method, you have to be very open-minded about change. Students may have made or lost progress over the summer, and it make take some rearranging to get the right groupings.

Goals

When implementing or assessing a reading program, you need aims, goals, and objectives. Not only is it important to the reading specialist, it is also important to the students. They need to know what is expected of them and what they should strive to accomplish. Aims are the broadest level. They are general statements that give the overall direction of the program. Aims are often not measurable. For example, the aim of the program may be to install a lifelong reading habit in the students. Goals are more specific and cover educational intent. A goal may be to give students the ability to guess at new words based on surrounding context. Finally, objectives are the most specific. An objective may be to read at least 500 pages by the end of a semester.

Intensive and extensive reading

When beginning a reading program, you need to know the difference between intensive reading and extensive reading. It is also important that your students know the difference and why each is important.

Balance

Every successful reading program has balance. You need the proper balance of extensive reading, intensive reading, vocabulary study, and so on to ensure that each area is addressed properly. Too much intensive reading will lead to a reader that lacks fluency. Too much extensive reading and a reader will lack

language skills. If vocabulary is neglected, reading development can be slow. The following percentages are recommended as guidelines: Intensive reading (grammar, vocabulary)—20%; independent vocabulary work (word study at home)—5-10%; skills and strategies (word families, background knowledge, inferential skills)—10-15%; extensive reading—55-65%.

Planning reading programs

When planning a reading program, there are a few things that are essential. First, make sure that everyone that will be involved in the reading program is also involved in the planning for it. Everyone should be involved in setting up the program. Decisions should be made as a group, and you should make sure that everyone understands each aspect of the program. Don't allow any one person to take too much responsibility. Also, do not push any standards upon teachers. It is a good idea to have broad standards and allow each teacher to make his or her own rules, such as how many pages are read, what is studied, and so on. If anyone else will be influenced by the program, let them know. Finally, make sure the students are aware of what is going on. Let them know the aims, goals, and objectives of the program.

Materials

Materials are obviously a vital part of any reading program. A good rule of thumb when beginning or maintaining a reading program is to obtain at least three books per student. The books must be at or just below the students' reading levels. You will need to gather materials on a variety of topics and at many levels. Do not assume that just because students are beginning readers, they all have beginning skills.

Book fairs and language conferences are good sources for scouting materials. Many times there will be free samples available. You should also check out any supplementary teaching materials that go with the books, such as vocabulary sheets, games, and other activities. These are also given away often.

Funding

Getting a reading program started requires quite a bit of funds. Many schools will have funds set up for starting such programs. For example, some schools will give teachers research funds that they can use to buy books. If this is the case, bulk-buying is a good option. It is usually the cheapest and it allows you to get a good variety of materials. Many educational companies also give discounts for such programs, so it is a good idea to check.

However, some schools must resort to external funds. Some teachers will ask each student to bring one book to class that they can read and share with others. You can also contact members of the community and local businesses for possible donations. Keep in mind, though, that getting enough books to start a program is only part of the problem. You will also need a constant source of funds to replace lost or damaged books and keep the selection updated.

Managing stock

Once you get enough books to begin a reading program, you need set up a system for their location, tracking, and use. Your school's library is the best location for keeping the program's books. If it is possible, use this option. However, many libraries are under-resourced and cannot handle the extra load. If this is the case, set up a simple system of your own. First, number each book. This is the easiest way to keep track of them. Next,

each book should be graded by level. Color-coding is a good way to do this. For example, yellow could be given to books with less than a 400 word level, red could be used for 400-750 word level books, and so on. Finally, you need a check-out system. The simplest way to do this is to have each student write down their name and the book number when they check out a book. When they are done, they put the book in a "drop box." Make sure that students do not swap books without going through the system.

Reading program assessments

When evaluating a reading program, there are two types of assessments that need to be done. First, you need to make assessments of the learners against the program's aims, goals, and objectives. There are many ways to do this. For example, you could give pass/fail grades for pages read, give higher grades for reading more material, grading reports, grading in-class performance and discussion, and grading improvements in reading speed. Second, you need to assess the reading program itself. Like anything else, the program needs to be evaluated and changed based on successes and needs. Make sure that everyone involved in the program is also involved in the assessment.

Selecting books

In order for a student to be a successful reader, he or she needs to be interested in the reading and the book cannot be too difficult. A good rule of thumb is that an appropriate book will have no more than three to five very difficult words or ideas for that student. A good book will also allow a reader to apply everything he or she knows about how words work with meaning.

If a book is too easy, they will not get a lot of work done. However, they are still getting in repetition. They need to see words and phrases many times in order to make recognition automatic. On the other hand, if the book is too difficult, they will be sacrificing meaning, words, and enjoyment. In the end, book selection is a combination of trial and error and expertise.

Modeling

In teaching, modeling refers to when a teacher shows students how to do something, not just instruct them. For example, a teacher will read aloud to students, then the students will repeat the reading themselves. The reason this is successful is because students can only give so much focus on extracting meaning from a text while reading. The same is true for teachers. Only so much can be gained by telling a teacher how they can make improvements. If teachers are struggling with adding a new concept, a reading specialist should show them how to apply that new concept by instructing the students as the teacher analyzes the instruction.

Teacher teaming

Teacher teaming involves teachers working together, as a "team," to instruct students. As a reading specialist, you need to be aware of the important aspects of successful team teaching. First, research has shown that teams are most effective when teachers of similar ages are paired together. This strategy should be used whenever possible. However, if only one specialist is available for an entire school, than age difference cannot be avoided. Second, teams should remain the same throughout the school year. This is not only good for continuity, but it also helps with planning. When planning instruction,

teams should strive to keep their planning as simple as possible. Planning by weeks is also advised.

Coaching

The goal of coaching teachers is to provide effective, ongoing, classroom-based development of instructors. Each school will have its own approach and strategies, but most successful coaching programs have things in common. These programs attempt to identify teacher needs and base help on developing those needs. Needs are addressed in a general manner so that they can be applied to every area of study. Successful coaching programs assess and approach the following needs: building relationships with students, effective assessment, planning and delivering instruction, meeting student needs, managing behavior, and gaining feedback.

Active listening

Establishing good communication with teachers and staff is vital for any reading specialist. One way to obtain good communication is to use a technique known as active listening. Many things can go wrong in communication if the speaker does not speak clearly or if the listener misinterprets the information. If listeners use their own words to repeat the communication, they are clarifying the message. This is known as active listening. For example, a teacher may say, "Josh isn't progressing with his decoding skills. I just don't know how to get through to him." An active listening response could be, "So you're instruction isn't working?" Such a response clarifies the meaning of the message. For example, if the teacher was speaking about his behavior and not the instruction, you would know immediately and the message would not be misinterpreted.

Factors inhibit listening

Since communication with staff members is so important, reading specialists should be aware of factors that hinder that communication. When speaking to other staff members, your message may not get through. In order to anticipate this, you need to be aware of factors that inhibit listening. Three common factors that hurt listening are bias, environmental factors, and response rehearsing. Bias can take many forms. Personal prejudice and anger are examples. Environmental factors, such as noise and temperature, also need to be taken into account. Finally, there is response rehearsing. Many times, a listener will only listen to the message long enough to form a response. Once they get enough information, they tune out the speaker and begin to think about what they will say next. Not only should you be aware of these factors as a speaker, but you should also keep them in mind when you are listening to other staff members. Good communication goes both ways.

Students' families

Establishing a positive relationship with students' families is essential for any reading specialist. While many parents are not involved in their children's education, it is not always their fault. Therefore, you need ways to reach out to them. The following tips help accomplish this:

- Send home parent surveys during the first week of school. These surveys should allow parents to give their thoughts on the reading program and help set up a foundation for positive communication.
- Make a positive phone call within the first nine weeks of school. This allows parents to become familiar with you and it lets them know they can contact you if they have any concerns.
- Send information home with students in weekly folders. This includes completed work, grades, and space for parents to voice their thoughts that they can send back with the students.
- Set up flexible hours for parent conferences. Show them they you are willing to make the extra effort to meet with them if they have any concerns or questions about their children or the reading program.

"I" messages

When communicating with colleagues, a reading specialist needs to be able to give constructive criticism and resolve conflict. Constructive criticism is the most effective when you give it in a relaxed manner. It allows you to communicate what behaviors and teaching methods can be improved upon. Constructive criticism is enhanced by using "I messages." I messages are a way to solve conflict without being aggressive. When giving an I message, use the following formula: I feel (how you feel) when (describe the event) because (how it effects you). For example, you may have an agreement with a teacher to get together once a week to discuss lesson plans, and this has not happened. You could say, "I feel concerned when you cancel your appointment because I think it could really help your instruction and your students."

Problem-solving

When there is a problem between staff members or with a part of the reading program, the best way to solve it is to use communication. The following model consists of six steps and is a good way to solve problems in a non-confrontational way.

- Step 1: Identify the problem. Use "I messages" to give your feelings, and allow the other person to share his or her feelings.
- Step 2: Determine the cause of the problem. What led to the problem? You need to both agree on the cause before moving to the next step.
- Step 3: Give possible solutions. Try to think of as many solutions to the problem as you can.
- Step 4: Analyze the solutions. Will they work? Why or why not? Narrow down the selection to a few possibilities.
- Step 5: Choose a solution. Both people should agree on a solution to try in which an effort is made by both. Put the plan into action.
- Step 6: Evaluate the results. Did the solution work or do we need to try again?

Reading specialists

It is important for a reading specialist to keep in contact with faculty and staff and inform them about current reading research and any changes you would like to make to the program. A good way to do this is to create a literacy newsletter that includes this information and is handed out to the school faculty and staff. The newsletter should be given out regularly, usually once each month, so that people may stay on top of the latest research for reading. It also gives the reading specialist a way to explain how he or she would like to use that research to implement changes in the reading program and increase its effectiveness.

Communicating with policymakers

As a reading specialist, you need to communicate with your elected officials

in order to gain support for reading education. There are many simple ways to do this, including the following:

- Pick up the phone. Make a call to your official's office and make contact with that person or his or her staff.
- Write. Send an e-mail or a letter to show how their decisions can impact reading education.
- Start a children's letter-writer campaign. Get your students to write letters to your elected officials. Let them hear the voices of the children their decisions affect.
- Publicize your reading program. Get the word out about reading education by contacting and involving your local media.

Inferential comprehension problems

A student who is having trouble with inferential comprehension likely is concentrating only on things that are explicitly stated. This causes him or her to miss out on main ideas and many cause-and-effect relationships. You could advise the teacher to give the student a reading-thinking activity. For example, the student would make predictions during reading. After making a prediction, he or she reads silently. When done, the teacher asks the student to confirm those predictions using examples from the reading. This technique is effective because making predictions gives the student a purpose for reading. It also forces them to make inferences based on their prior knowledge.

Comprehension and vocabulary problems

While the student shows phonological awareness and good decoding skills, he or she still needs help with comprehension and increasing vocabulary. You should recommend strategies to help the student apply self-monitoring skills and increase his or her independent reading.

To help with self-monitoring skills, the teacher should give guided reading practice that includes asking questions while reading. The student needs to be prompted to make connections between the text and his or her own experiences and knowledge. Checklists will also help the student self-monitor comprehension during independent work.

You should also advise the teacher to increase the student's independent reading. Independent reading will help increase vocabulary and also reinforce self-monitoring techniques by giving him or her chance to practice such skills.

Important Terms

Consonant blends—A Sequence of consonants that occur before or after a vowel in the same syllable. Examples are "cl" and "st." Sometimes consonant blends are referred to as blends.

Consonant digraphs—Combination of letters that make one sound, but that one sound is not represented by any of the letters by themselves. Examples are "th" and "ph."

Derivation—Process of word formation that involves adding a derivational affix to a word to form a new word. Usually, the addition changes the words syntactic function. For example, adding "-ly" changes an adjective to an adverb (quick to quickly).

Inflection—Inflection refers to the modification of a word to describe that word, such as tense, number, person, or gender. For example, adding the inflection –ed to a word usually makes it past tense (call to called).

Semantic cues—Support given by the meanings of written or spoken words that help a person identify an unknown word.

Semantic properties—Features that make up the meaning of a word.

Syntactic cues—Support given by language rules that help a person identify a word based on how it is used in grammar.

Syntax—Study of sentence structure or the rules for how sentences are formed.

Vowel patterns—Combination of vowels that, when put together, create a single vowel sound. An example is the "oa" combination in the word "load." Vowel patterns are also called vowel combinations, vowel digraphs, vowel pairs, and vowel teams.

Word origins—Refers to how a word came to be. Words can originate from borrowing, formation, and sound symbolism. Borrowing refers to the taking of a word from another language. Formation describes the forming of words from derivations, compounding, and so on. Sound symbolism is creation of words that are similar to existing words.

Practice Test

Practice Questions

1. Sea and *see*, *fair* and *fare*, are called:
- a. Homophones
- b. Antonyms
- c. Homophobes
- d. Twin words

2. Another name for a persuasive essay is:
- a. Dynamic essay
- b. Convincing essay
- c. Argumentative essay
- d. Position paper

3. A teacher is working with a group of third graders at the same reading level. Her goal is to improve reading fluency. She asks each child in turn to read a page from a book about mammal young. She asks the children to read with expression. She also reminds them they don't need to stop between each word; they should read as quickly as they comfortably can. She cautions them, however, not to read so quickly that they leave out or misread a word. The teacher knows the components of reading fluency are:
- a. Speed, drama, and comprehension
- b. Cohesion, rate, and prosody
- c. Understanding, rate, and prosody
- d. Rate, accuracy, and prosody

4. "Language load" refers to:
- a. The basic vocabulary words a first grader has committed to memory.
- b. The number of unrecognizable words an English Language Learner encounters when reading a passage or listening to a teacher.
- c. The damage that carrying a pile of heavy books could cause to a child's physique.
- d. The number of different languages a person has mastered.

5. A syllable must contain:
- a. A vowel
- b. A consonant
- c. Both a vowel and a consonant
- d. A meaning

6. A third-grade teacher has several students reading above grade level. Most of the remaining students are reading at grade level. There are also a few students reading below grade level. She decides to experiment. Her hypothesis is that by giving the entire class a chapter book above grade level, high-level readers will be satisfied, grade-level readers will be challenged in a positive way, and students reading below grade level will be inspired to improve. Her method is most likely to:

    a. Succeed, producing students reading at an Instructional reading level. High-level readers will be happy to be given material appropriate to their reading level. Grade-level readers will challenge themselves to improve reading strategies in order to master the text. Because only a few of the students are reading below grade level, the other students, who feel happy and energized, will inspire the slower readers by modeling success.

    b. Succeed, producing students reading at an Independent reading level. High-level readers will independently help grade-level readers who will, in turn, independently help those below grade level.

    c. Fail, producing students at a Frustration reading level. Those reading below grade level are likely to give up entirely. Those reading at grade level are likely to get frustrated and form habits that will actually slow down their development.

    d. Fail, producing students reading at a Chaotic reading level. By nature, children are highly competitive. The teacher has not taken into consideration multiple learning styles. The children who are at grade level will either become bitter and angry at those whose reading level is above grade level or simply give up. The children reading below grade level will not be able to keep up and will in all likelihood act out their frustration or completely shut down.

7. Of the three tiers of words, the most important words for direct instruction are:

    a. Tier-one words
    b. Common words
    c. Tier-two words
    d. Words with Latin roots

8. At the beginning of each month, Mr. Yi has Jade read a page or two from a book she hasn't seen before. He notes the total number of words in the section, and also notes the number of times she leaves out or misreads a word. If Jade reads the passage with less than 3% error, Mr. Yi is satisfied that Jade is:

    a. Reading with full comprehension.
    b. Probably bored and should try a more difficult book.
    c. Reading at her Independent reading level.
    d. Comfortable with the syntactical meaning.

9. The purpose of corrective feedback is:

    a. To provide students with methods for explaining to the teacher or classmates what a passage was about.

    b. To correct an error in reading a student has made, specifically clarifying where and how the error was made so that the student can avoid similar errors in the future.

    c. To provide a mental framework that will help the student correctly organize new information.

    d. To remind students that error is essential in order to truly understand and that it is not something to be ashamed of.

10. Dr. Jenks is working with a group of high school students. They are about to read a science book about fossils. Before they begin, she writes the words *stromatolites, fossiliferous,* and *eocene* on the board. She explains the meaning of each word. These words are examples of:
    a. Academic words
    b. Alliteration
    c. Content-specific words
    d. Ionization

11. Which of the following best explains the importance prior knowledge brings to the act of reading?
    a. Prior knowledge is information the student gets through researching a topic prior to reading the text. A student who is well-prepared through such research is better able to decode a text and retain its meaning.
    b. Prior knowledge is knowledge the student brings from previous life or learning experiences to the act of reading. It is not possible for a student to fully comprehend new knowledge without first integrating it with prior knowledge.
    c. Prior knowledge is predictive. It motivates the student to look for contextual clues in the reading and predict what is likely to happen next.
    d. Prior knowledge is not important to any degree to the act of reading, because every text is self-contained and therefore seamless. Prior knowledge is irrelevant in this application.

12. A cloze test evaluates a student's:
    a. Reading fluency.
    b. Understanding of context and vocabulary.
    c. Phonemic skills.
    d. Ability to apply the alphabetic principle to previously unknown material.

13. Sight words are:
    a. Common words with irregular spelling.
    b. Words that can easily be found on educational websites.
    c. Any word that can be seen, including text words, words on signs, brochures, banners, and so forth.
    d. There is no such thing; because oral language is learned before written language, all words are ultimately based on sound. The correct term is sound words and includes all words necessary to decode a particular text.

14. *Phone, they, church.* The underlined letters in these words are examples of:
    a. Consonant blend
    b. Consonant shift
    c. Continental shift
    d. Consonant digraph

15. Phonemic awareness is a type of:
    a. Phonological awareness. Phonemic awareness is the ability to recognize sounds within words.
    b. Phonics. It is a teaching technique whereby readers learn the relationship between letters and sounds.
    c. Alphabetization. Unless a reader knows the alphabet, phonemic awareness is useless.
    d. Syntactical awareness. Understanding the underlying structure of a sentence is key to understanding meaning.

16. All members of a group of kindergarten students early in the year are able to chant the alphabet. The teacher is now teaching the students what the alphabet looks like in written form. The teacher points to a letter and the students vocalize the correspondent sound. Alternatively, the teacher vocalizes a phoneme and a student points to it on the alphabet chart. The teacher is using _____ in her instruction.
    a. Letter–sound correspondence
    b. Rote memorization
    c. Predictive analysis
    d. Segmentation

17. A fourth-grade teacher is preparing her students for a reading test in which a number of words have been replaced with blanks. The test will be multiple-choice; there are three possible answers given for each blank. The teacher instructs the children to read all the possible answers and cross out any answer that obviously doesn't fit. Next, the students should "plug in" the remaining choices and eliminate any that are grammatically incorrect or illogical. Finally, the student should consider contextual clues in order to select the best answer. This in an example of:
    a. Strategy instruction
    b. Diagnostic instruction
    c. Skills instruction
    d. Multiple-choice instruction

18. The term "common words" means:
    a. One-syllable words with fewer than three letters. Some examples are it, an, a, I, go, to, and in. They are the first words an emergent writer learns.
    b. One-syllable words with fewer than five letters. Some examples include sing, goes, sit, rock, walk, and took.
    c. Words that are ordinary or unexceptional; because they tend to flatten a piece of writing, they should be avoided.
    d. Familiar, frequently used words that do not need to be taught beyond primary grades.

19. Which is greater, the number of English phonemes or the number of letters in the alphabet?
    a. The number of letters in the alphabet, because they can be combined to create phonemes.
    b. The number of phonemes. A phoneme is the smallest measure of language sound.

    c. They are identical; each letter "owns" a correspondent sound.
    d. Neither. Phonemes and alphabet letters are completely unrelated.

20. *Train, brain, spring.* The underlined letters are examples of:
    a. Consonant digraph
    b. Consonant blend
    c. Consonant shift
    d. Continental shift

21. It is the beginning of the school year. To determine which second-grade students might need support, the reading teacher wants to identify those who are reading below grade level. She works with students one at a time. She gives each child a book at a second-grade reading level and asks the child to read out loud for two minutes. Children who will need reading support are those who read:
    a. Fewer than 100 words in the time given.
    b. Fewer than 200 words in the time given.
    c. More than 75 words in the time given.
    d. The entire book in the time given.

22. The most effective strategy for decoding sight words is:
    a. Segmenting sight words into syllables. Beginning readers are understandably nervous when encountering a long word that isn't familiar. Blocking off all but a single syllable at a time renders a word manageable and allows the reader a sense of control over the act of reading.
    b. Word families. By grouping the sight word with similar words, patterns emerge.
    c. A phonemic approach. When students understand the connection between individual words and their sounds, they will be able to sound out any sight word they encounter.
    d. None; sight words cannot be decoded. Readers must learn to recognize these words as wholes on sight.

23. The reading teacher is working with a group of English Language Learners. Which of the following strategies will help these students learn to read with enhanced fluency?
    a. The teacher reads aloud while students follow the words in their books.
    b. Tape-assisted reading.
    c. Having the students' parents or another trustworthy adult read with the child each evening for 45 minutes.
    d. A and B.

24. "Decoding" is also called:
    a. Remediation
    b. Deciphering
    c. Alphabetic principle
    d. Deconstruction

25. A reading teacher is working with a group of English Language Learners. She has asked them to study sequentially the pictures in a storybook and then tell her what they think the story is about. This approach will help the students understand the _____ of the story.
    a. Theme

b. Context
c. Events
d. Deeper meaning

26. Phonological awareness activities are:
    a. Oral
    b. Visual
    c. Both A and B
    d. Semantically based

27. A student is able to apply strategies to comprehend the meanings of unfamiliar words; can supply definitions for words with several meanings such as *crucial, criticism,* and *witness*; and is able to reflect on her background knowledge in order to decipher a word's meaning. These features of effective reading belong to which category?
    a. Word recognition
    b. Vocabulary
    c. Content
    d. Comprehension

28. A reading teacher is assessing an eighth grader to determine her reading level. Timed at a minute, the student reads with 93% accuracy. She misreads an average of seven words out of 100. What is her reading level?
    a. She is reading at a Frustration level.
    b. She is reading at an Excellence level.
    c. She is reading at an Instructional level.
    d. She is reading at an Independent level.

29. When should students learn how to decode?
    a. Decoding is the most basic and essential strategy to becoming a successful reader. It should be introduced to kindergartners during the first two weeks of school.
    b. Decoding is not a teachable skill. It is an unconscious act and is natural to all learners.
    c. Decoding should be taught only after children have mastered every letter–sound relationship as well as every consonant digraph and consonant blend. They should also be able to recognize and say the 40 phonemes common to English words and be able to recognize at least a dozen of the most common sight words.
    d. Decoding depends on an understanding of letter–sound relationships. As soon as a child understands enough letters and their correspondent sounds to read a few words, decoding should be introduced.

30. *Since, whether,* and *accordingly* are examples of which type of signal words?
    a. Common, or basic, signal words
    b. Compare/contrast words
    c. Cause–effect words
    d. Temporal sequencing words

31. A class is reading *The Heart Is a Lonely Hunter*. The teacher asks students to write a short paper explaining the story's resolution. She is asking them to locate and discuss the story's:
    a. Outcome

    b. Highest or most dramatic moment
    c. Plot
    d. Lowest point

32. A student encounters a multisyllabic word. She's not sure if she's seen it before. What should she do first? What should she do next?
    a. Locate familiar word parts, then locate the consonants.
    b. Locate the consonants, then locate the vowels.
    c. Locate the vowels, then locate familiar word parts.
    d. Look it up in the dictionary, then write down the meaning.

Read the following story, then answer the questions that follow:

The kindergarten teacher is concerned about three of her students. While they are enthusiastic about writing, they do not always recognize letters, confusing b, d, and p, or e and o. They do, however, know which sounds go with certain letters when they are orally drilled. When they write, they appear to be attempting letter–sound associations.

"Now I'm writing *M*," the teacher heard one boy say as he scripted a large *N* in the upper right corner of his paper. He studied it for a moment and added, "Nope, it needs another leg." The student then wrote an *I* beside the *N*. "There," he said. "Now you are an *M*. I can write the word, 'man,' because now I have *M*." The child then moved to the lower left corner of the paper. "M-A-N," he said to himself, slowly pronouncing each sound. "I already have that *M*. Here is where the rest of the word goes." He turned the paper sideways and wrote *N*.

The second child sang to herself as she gripped the crayon and scribbled lines here and there on her paper. Some of the lines resembled letters, but few actually were. Others were scribbles. As she "wrote," she seemed to be making up a story and seemed to believe she was writing the story down.

The third child didn't vocalize at all while he worked. He gripped the paper and carefully wrote the same letter over and over and over. Sometimes the letter was large, sometimes tiny. He turned the paper in every direction so that sometimes the letter was sideways or upside down. Sometimes he flipped it backward. "What are you writing?" the teacher asked him. "My name," the child told her. The teacher then realized the letter was, indeed, the first letter of his name. She gently told him he had done a fine job of writing the first letter of his name. Did he want her to help him write the rest of it? "Nope," he cheerfully told her, "it's all here." He pointed at one of the letters and "read" his full name. He pointed at another letter and again seemed to believe it represented all the sounds of his name.

33. The kindergarten teacher isn't certain if these children are exhibiting signs of a reading disability or other special needs. What should the teacher do?
   a. Nothing. These children are simply at an early stage in the reading/writing process.
   b. Nothing. She doesn't want to have to tell the parents that their children are sub-par in terms of intelligence. They are perfectly nice children and can contribute to society in other ways. She resolves to give them extra attention in other areas to help them build confidence.
   c. She should recommend that the parents take the children to be tested for a number of reading disorders, including dyslexia.
   d. She should arrange a meeting between herself, the school psychologist, and the reading specialist to discuss the matter and resolve it using a three-pronged approach.

34. In the above example, the emergent writers are demonstrating their understanding that letters symbolize predictable sounds, that words begin with an initial sound/letter, and that by "writing," they are empowering themselves by offering a reader access to their thoughts and ideas. The next three stages the emergent writers will pass through in order will most likely be:
   a. Scripting the end-sound to a word (KT=cat); leaving space between words; writing from the top left to the top right of the page, and from top to bottom.
   b. Scripting the end-sound to a word (KT=cat); writing from the top left to the top right of the page, and from top to bottom; separating the words from one another with a space between.
   c. Leaving space between the initial letters that represent words; writing from the top left to the top right of the page, and from top to bottom; scripting the final sound of each word as well as the initial sound (KT=cat).
   d. Drawing a picture beside each of the initial sounds to represent the entire word; scripting the end-sound to a word (KT=cat); scripting the interior sounds that compose the entire word (KAT=cat).

35. The teacher might best encourage the three students in the above example by:
   a. Suggesting they write an entire book rather than just a single page. This will build confidence, teach them sequencing, and encourage the young writers to delve deeper into their ideas.
   b. Ask the students to read their stories to her. Suggest they visit other children in the class and read to each of them.
   c. Contact the local newspaper and invite a reporter to visit her class and write a story about her emergent writers. In this way, they are sure to see themselves as "real writers" and will more fully apply themselves to the task.
   d. Invite all the parents to visit the class the following week. This will give all classmates, regardless of where they are on the learning spectrum, time to memorize their stories. The children will be very excited and will begin to see themselves as "real writers."

36. At what point should the kindergarten teacher in the above example offer the three children picture books and ask them to read to her?
   a. When the three children are all able to script initial sounds, end sounds, and interior sounds they are ready to decode words. She should make her request at this point.
   b. As each child reaches the stage in which he or she can script initial sounds, end sounds, and interior sounds, the teacher should ask only that child to read to her.
   c. As each child reaches the stage in which he habitually writes from the top to the bottom of the page, moving left to right, the time has come. Books are intended to be read in this way, and until a child has had the experience of writing in the same manner, he won't be able to make sense of the words.
   d. The teacher should encourage all students to "read" picture books from the first day of school. Talking about the pictures from page to page gives young readers the idea that books are arranged sequentially. Pictures also offer narrative coherence and contextual clues. Emergent readers who are encouraged to enjoy books will more readily embrace the act of reading. Holding a book and turning pages gives young readers a familiarity with them.

37. How does a teacher most effectively teach spelling?
   a. Students who have a clear understanding of letter–sound association do not need to be taught to spell. If they can say a word, they can spell it.
   b. Students who have a clear understanding of letter–sound association, who can identify syllables, and who recognize when the base word is of Latin, Greek, or Indo-European ancestry do not need to be taught to spell. They can deduce what is most likely the correct spelling using a combination of these strategies. A teacher who posts charts organizing words into their ancestor families, phonemic units, and word-sound families is efficiently teaching spelling. The rest is up to the student.
   c. Students who spell poorly will be at a disadvantage for the rest of their lives. It is essential that students spend at least 15 minutes a day drilling spelling words until they know them forward and backward. The teacher should alternate between having students write a new word 25 times and having the entire class chant the spelling of the words.
   d. Students should be taught that writing is a process. By teaching students to apply spelling patterns found in common phonemic units, the spelling of many words can be deduced. Sight words that are high frequency and do not follow patterns found in other words (the, guardian, colonel) must be taught.

38. A teacher is teaching students analogizing. She is teaching them to:
   a. Identify and use metaphors.
   b. Identify and use similes.
   c. Identify and use groups of letters that occur in a word family.
   d. Identify and use figures of speech.

39. A reading teacher is working with a student who has just moved to Texas from Korea. The child knows very few words in English. The teacher offers her a picture book of Korean folk tales. Using words and gestures, the teacher asks her to "read" one folk tale. The child "reads" the familiar tale in Korean. The teacher then writes key English words on the board and asks the child to find those words in the book. When the child finds the words, they read them together. This strategy is:
   a. Useful. The child will feel more confident because the story is already familiar. She will also feel that the lesson is a conversation of sorts, and that she is communicating successfully. She will be motivated to learn the English words because they are meaningful and highly charged.
   b. Useful. The teacher is learning as much as the child is. The teacher is learning about Korean culture and language, and she can apply this knowledge when teaching future Korean students.
   c. Not very useful. The child needs to be exposed to as much American culture as possible. Encouraging her to remember her own culture will make her sad and will limit her curiosity about her new home.
   d. Not very useful. The first things the child should learn are the letters of the alphabet and associative sounds. Only then can she begin to decipher an unfamiliar language.

40. The teacher in the previous question was using what kind of load?
   a. Language load
   b. Cognitive load
   c. Bilingual load
   d. Cultural load

41. Using brain imaging, researchers have discovered that dyslexic readers use the _____ side(s) of their brains, while non-dyslexic readers use the _____ side(s) of their brains.
   a. Left; right
   b. Right; left
   c. Right and left; left
   d. Right; left and right

42. A fifth grader has prepared a report on reptiles, which is something he knows a great deal about. He rereads his report and decides to make a number of changes. He moves a sentence from the top to the last paragraph. He crosses out several words and replaces them with more specific words. He circles key information and draws an arrow to show another place the information could logically be placed. He is engaged in:
   a. Editing
   b. Revising
   c. First editing, then revising
   d. Reviewing

43. *Bi, re,* and *un* are:
   a. Suffixes, appearing at the beginning of base words to change their meaning.
   b. Suffixes, appearing at the end of base words to enhance their meaning.
   c. Prefixes, appearing at the beginning of base words to emphasize their meaning.
   d. Prefixes, appearing at the beginning of base words to change their meanings.

44. Examples of CVC words include:
 a. Add, pad, mad
 b. Cat, tack, act
 c. Elephant, piano, examine
 d. Dog, sit, leg

45. A teacher is working with a student who is struggling with reading. The teacher gives him a story with key words missing:

> The boy wanted to take the dog for a walk. The boy opened the door. The ____ ran out. The ___ looked for the dog. When he found the dog, he was very _____.

The student is able to fill in the blanks by considering:
 a. Syntax. Oftentimes, word order gives enough clues that a reader can predict what happens next.
 b. Pretext. By previewing the story, the student can deduce the missing words.
 c. Context. By considering the other words in the story, the student can determine the missing words.
 d. Sequencing. By putting the ideas in logical order, the student can determine the missing words.

46. The following is/are (an) element(s) of metacognition:
 a. A reader's awareness of herself as a learner.
 b. A reader's understanding of a variety of reading strategies and how to apply them to comprehend a text.
 c. A reader who is conscious about remembering what has been read.
 d. All of the above.

47. Collaborative Strategic Reading (CSR) is a teaching technique that depends on two teaching practices. These practices are:
 a. Cooperative learning and reading comprehension.
 b. Cooperative reading and metacognition.
 c. Reading comprehension and metacognition.
 d. Cooperative learning and metacognition.

48. Context cues are useful in:
 a. Predicting future action.
 b. Understanding the meaning of words that are not familiar.
 c. Understanding character motivation.
 d. Reflecting on a text's theme.

49. A teacher has a child who does not volunteer in class. When the teacher asks the student a question the student can answer, she does so with as few words as possible. The teacher isn't sure how to best help the child. She should:
   a. Leave the child alone. She is clearly very shy and will be embarrassed by having attention drawn to her. She is learning in her own way.
   b. Ask two or three highly social children to include this girl in their activities. She is shy, and she probably won't approach them on her own.
   c. Observe the child over the course of a week or two. Draw her into conversation and determine if her vocabulary is limited, if she displays emotional problems, or if her reticence could have another cause. Note how the child interacts with others in the class. Does she ever initiate conversation? If another child initiates, does she respond?
   d. Refer her to the school counselor immediately. It is clear the child is suffering from either a low IQ or serious problems at home.

50. A first grader is reading a book aloud. The teacher notes that the book uses word families. Some of the words are *fat, hat, sat, fit, hit, sit, run, fun, sun, hot, cot,* and *not.* The child ignores the pictures and attempts to read by identifying the rhyme. However, she frequently misreads, replacing the correct word with another from the same word family. The child needs:
   a. Encouragement. She will eventually understand.
   b. Intervention. She can identify groups of letters, but is not able to apply letter–sound association.
   c. To practice singing the alphabet.
   d. Nothing. This is a normal stage in the reading process.

51. A high school class reads an essay about the possible effects of sexual activity on teens. The author's position is very clear: She believes young people should avoid sex because they aren't mature enough to take the necessary steps to remain safe. The author cites facts, research studies, and statistics to strengthen her position. This type of writing is called:
   a. Expository
   b. Narrative
   c. Persuasive
   d. Didactic

52. A reading teacher feels that some of his strategies aren't effective. He has asked a specialist to observe him and make suggestions as to how he can improve. The reading specialist should suggest that first:
   a. The teacher set up a video camera and record several sessions with different students for the specialist to review. The presence of an observer changes the outcome; if the specialist is in the room, it will negatively affect the students' ability to read.
   b. The teacher reflect on his strategies himself. Which seem to work? Which don't? Can the teacher figure out why? It's always best to encourage teachers to find their own solutions so that they can handle future issues themselves.
   c. They meet to discuss areas the teacher is most concerned about and decide on the teacher's goals.
   d. The specialist should arrive unannounced to observe the teacher interacting with students. This will prevent the teacher from unconsciously overpreparing.

53. A kindergarten teacher pronounces a series of word pairs for her students. The students repeat the pairs. Some of the pairs rhyme (*see/bee*) and some of the pairs share initial sounds but do not rhyme (*sit, sun*). The students help her separate the word pairs into pairs that rhyme and pairs that do not. Once the students are able to distinguish between two words that rhyme and two words that do not, the teacher says a word and asks them to provide a rhyme. When she says *cat* a child responds with *fat*. When she says *sing* a child offers *thing*. How does this strictly oral activity contribute to the children's ability to read?
   a. It doesn't. Oral activities must have a written component to be useful to emergent readers.
   b. It is helpful in that it demonstrates how different sounds are made with different letters.
   c. It actually discourages children from reading. By emphasizing orality over literacy, the teacher is suggesting to the children that reading is not an important skill.
   d. Being able to identify rhyme is an important element of phonological awareness.

54. Syllable types include:
   a. Closed, open, silent e, vowel team, vowel-r, and consonant-le.
   b. Closed, open, silent, double-vowel, r, and le.
   c. Closed, midway, open, emphasized, prefixed, and suffixed.
   d. Stressed, unstressed, and silent.

55. An eighth-grade student is able to decode most words fluently and has a borderline/acceptable vocabulary, but his reading comprehension is quite low. He can be helped with instructional focus on:
   a. Strategies to increase comprehension and to build vocabulary.
   b. Strategies to increase comprehension and to be able to identify correct syntactical usage.
   c. Strategies to improve his understanding of both content and context.
   d. Strategies to build vocabulary and to improve his understanding of both content and context.

56. Reading comprehension and vocabulary can best be assessed:
   a. With brief interviews and tests every two months to determine how much learning has taken place. Students learn in spurts, and in-depth assessments of comprehension and vocabulary are a waste of time.
   b. Through a combination of standardized testing, informal teacher observations, attention to grades, objective-linked assessments, and systematized charting of data over time.
   c. By giving students weekly self-assessment rubrics to keep them constantly aware of and invested in their own progress.
   d. By having students retell a story or summarize the content of an informational piece of writing. The degree to which the material was comprehended, and the richness or paucity of vocabulary used in such work, provides efficient and thorough assessment.

57. An ORF is:
   a. An Oral Reading Fluency assessment.
   b. An Occasional Reading Function assessment.

    c.   An Oscar Reynolds Feinstein assessment.

    d.   An Overt Reading Failure assessment.

58. An outcome assessment is given:
    a.   At the end of the year, to determine if instructional goals established at the beginning of the year have been successfully reached.
    b.   At the beginning of the year to establish a point of reference for a series of regularly administered assessments throughout the year.
    c.   When a student has finished a text to determine how clearly she understood the story's implied outcome.
    d.   There is no such assessment.

59. Word-recognition ability is:
    a.   Equally important to all readers.
    b.   Used only by fluent readers.
    c.   Another term for "word attack."
    d.   Especially important to English Language Learners and students with reading disabilities.

60. Research indicates that developing oral language proficiency in emergent readers is important because:
    a.   Proficiency with oral language enhances students' phonemic awareness and increases vocabulary.
    b.   The more verbally expressive emergent readers are, the more confident they become. Such students will embrace both Academic and Independent reading levels.
    c.   It encourages curiosity about others. With strong oral language skills, students begin to question the world around them. The more they ask, the richer their background knowledge.
    d.   It demonstrates to students that their ideas are important and worth sharing.

61. In preparation for writing a paper, a high school class has been instructed to skim a number of Internet and print documents. They are being asked to:
    a.   Read the documents several times, skimming to a deeper level of understanding each time.
    b.   Read the documents quickly, looking for those that offer the most basic, general information.
    c.   Read the documents quickly, looking for key words in order to gather the basic premise of each.
    d.   Read the documents carefully, looking for those that offer the most in-depth information.

62. The students in the above question are most likely preparing to write a(n) _____ essay:
    a.   Personal
    b.   Expository
    c.   Literary
    d.   Narrative

A teacher has given the first paragraph of an essay to her students to analyze and discuss. Read the paragraph and answer the following questions:

> Americans have struggled with cigarettes far too long. Until now, it has been a personal choice to smoke (or not), but the time for change is rapidly approaching. Local legislation has already begun for schools, restaurants, arenas, and other public places to be smoke-free. Years ago cigarette smoking was presented by the media as being fashionable, even sexy. In magazines, movies, and later in television, celebrities would indulge themselves with a smoke and even be paid to endorse a brand. As recently as 1975, it was common for talk show hosts like Tom Snyder and Johnny Carson to keep a cigarette burning. Cigarette smoking in America has persisted in spite of frightening concerns like lung cancer and emphysema. Over the years, the tobacco industry has sought to diffuse strong evidence that smoking is harmful. However, the myth of "safe cigarettes," questions about nicotine addiction, and denials about the dangers of secondhand smoke have proven to be propaganda and lies.

63. This is a(n) _____ essay:
    a. Compare/contrast
    b. Persuasive
    c. Narrative
    d. Analytic

64. The thesis statement is:
    a. However, the myth of "safe cigarettes," questions about nicotine addiction, and denials about the dangers of secondhand smoke have proven to be propaganda and lies.
    b. Americans have struggled with cigarettes far too long.
    c. Until now, it has been a personal choice to smoke (or not), but the time for change is rapidly approaching.
    d. In magazines, movies, and later in television, celebrities would indulge themselves with a smoke and even be paid to endorse a brand.

65. The next three paragraphs in the essay will most likely address:
    a. Smoking as a personal choice, changes in local legislation, and how fashionable smoking once was.
    b. How fashionable smoking once was, talk show hosts smoking on air, the myth of "safe cigarettes."
    c. Propaganda and lies, the myth of "safe cigarettes," and how long Americans have struggled with cigarettes.
    d. The myth of "safe cigarettes," questions about nicotine addiction, and the dangers of secondhand smoke.

66. The teacher and her students brainstorm a list of talents, skills, and specialized knowledge belonging to members of the class. Some of the items on the list include how to make a soufflé, how to juggle, and how to teach a dog to do tricks. One student knows a great deal about spiders, and another about motorcycles. She asks each student to write an

essay about something he or she is good at or knows a great deal about. What kind of essay is she asking the students to produce?

a. Cause and effect
b. Compare/contrast
c. Example
d. Argumentative

67. *Caret, carrot, to, two and too* share something in common. They:

a. Are nouns.
b. Are monosyllabic.
c. Are homophones.
d. Represent things in nature.

Read the following paragraph, then answer the questions that follow:

> A class will visit an assisted living facility to interview residents about their lives. Each group of three has selected a theme such as love, work, or personal accomplishment and written several questions around that theme. Next, each group practices interviewing one another. The teacher then asks all the students to discuss the questions that caused them to respond most thoughtfully, as well as those they were less inspired by. The students decided the questions that were easiest to respond to asked for very specific information; for example, one inspiring question was, "Please tell me about something you learned to do as a child that affected the direction of your life." Those that were uninspiring were too broad, for example, "Please tell me about your happiest memory."

68. After they interview the residents, each group of three students will work together to write a piece about the resident. This kind of approach is called:

a. Collaborative learning
b. Companion learning
c. Bonded learning
d. Group learning

69. The genre the teacher expects is:

a. Memoir
b. Historical fiction
c. Biography
d. Autobiography

70. The teacher wants the students to apply what they've learned across content areas. Which of the following strategies would be most effective?

a. Students will interview a family member, asking the same questions.
b. Students will write a personal piece in which they address the same questions.
c. Students will do online research about the cultural, economic, or political events that were occurring during the specific time about which they've written.
d. Students pretend to be the interviewee and rewrite the piece from a first person point of view.

Read the following paragraph, and then respond to the questions that follow.

A seventh-grade teacher asks the reading teacher to suggest a lesson students will find simultaneously challenging and fun. The reading teacher suggests the class read fairy tales from both Hans Christian Anderson and the Brothers Grimm and have a rapid-paced, energetic discussion about the many similarities and differences between the two while the teacher lists them on the board.

71. The individual strategies the students will employ are:
    a. Collaborative learning and genre.
    b. Brainstorming and a compare/contrast strategy.
    c. Collaborative learning and brainstorming.
    d. Analyzing and genre.

72. The lesson is asking the students to consider two different:
    a. Learning styles
    b. Genres
    c. Writing styles
    d. Reading styles

73. The primary benefit of this exercise is that it promotes students':
    a. Vocabulary
    b. Comprehension
    c. Fluency
    d. Word identification

74. The students enjoyed the assignment so much that the teacher suggested they select one fairy tale and modernize it without changing the basic structure. Evil kings and queens could become corrupt politicians; pumpkins could turn into Hummers, and romantic princes might reveal themselves as rock stars. The teacher believes this assignment will most effectively demonstrate to the students:
    a. The importance of setting to meaning.
    b. The importance of characters to meaning.
    c. The importance of culture to meaning.
    d. The importance of creativity to meaning.

75. The first-grade teacher wants her class to understand that stories have a certain order. She reads them a story, then orally reviews with them how each event that happened in the story caused the next event to happen. To reinforce the lesson the teacher should:
   a. Give each child a piece of drawing paper that has been folded in half and then again, creating four boxes, along with a piece that has not been folded. The teacher should then ask the students to draw a cartoon about the story. Each of the first four boxes will show the events in order. The second page is to show how the story ends.
   b. Give each child a piece of drawing paper and ask the students to draw the most important scene.
   c. Give each child a piece of drawing paper and ask the students to draw the story's beginning on the front of the page and ending on the back.
   d. Give each child a piece of drawing paper that has been folded in half and then again, creating four boxes, along with a piece that has not been folded. The teacher should then ask the students to draw a cartoon about anything they want. She reminds them to put their story cartoons in proper order.

76. A ninth grade class is reading a 14-line poem in iambic pentameter. There are three stanzas of four lines each, and a two-line couplet at the end. Words at the end of each line rhyme with another word in the same stanza. The class is reading a:
   a. Sonnet
   b. Villanelle
   c. Sestina
   d. Limerick

77. A teacher is working with a group of English Language Learners. She asks them to take two pieces of paper. At the top of the first paper they are to write *SAME*. At the top of the other, *DIFFERENT.* Each child will consider what his native country and the United States have in common, and what distinct features each country possesses. The children are using which method in organizing their ideas?
   a. Hunt and peck
   b. Consider and persuade
   c. Evaluate and contrast
   d. Compare and contrast

78. Next, the teacher in the previous story drew two overlapping circles on the board. She labeled one circle *MALI.* The other circle was labeled *U.S.* She labeled the overlap joining the two circles *SAME.* On the far side of each circle, she wrote *DIFFERENT.* In the *U.S.* circle, she wrote *many cars, very good roads, people live in big cities, many families have pets,* and *houses made of wood.* In the side labeled *MALI* she wrote *fewer cars, many broken roads, most people live in villages, animals are not pets,* and *houses made of mud.* What will she write in the third, overlapping area?
   a. Telephones, personal computers, cars, and apartment buildings.
   b. Dogs, cats, fish, and birds.
   c. People celebrate marriages, births, and historical events.
   d. Movies, *television, books,* and *Internet.*

79. What type of prewriting activity has the teacher in the previous example drawn on the board?
   a. A verbal diagram
   b. Thought bubbles
   c. A web
   d. A Venn diagram

80. A third grader knows he needs to write from left to right, and from top to bottom on the page. He knows what sounds are associated with specific letters. He can recognize individual letters and can hear word families. He correctly identifies prefixes, suffixes, and homonyms, and his reading comprehension is very good. However, when he is asked to write, he becomes very upset. He has trouble holding a pencil, his letters are very primitively executed, and his written work is not legible. He most likely has:
   a. Dysgraphia
   b. Dyslexia
   c. Dyspraxia
   d. Nonverbal learning disorder

81. The phrase "Pretty as a picture" is *best* described as a:
   a. Metaphor
   b. Cliché
   c. Simile
   d. Figure of speech

82. A fourth-grade teacher had her students write haiku in order to promote the students' _____.
   a. Reading comprehension
   b. Vocabulary
   c. Word identification skills
   d. Confidence

83. A second-grade teacher wants to help her students enrich their vocabulary. She's noticed that their writing journals are filled with serviceable but unexciting verbs such as "said" and "went," and general rather than specific nouns. The most effective lesson would involve:
   a. Suggesting students use a thesaurus to substitute more unusual words for common ones.
   b. Suggesting students add an adjective to each noun.
   c. Brainstorming a list of verbs that mean ways of talking or ways of going, then adding them to the word wall along with some nouns that specify common topics.
   d. Suggesting students look up the meanings of boring words and consider another way to express them.

84. At the beginning of the school year, a parent is concerned about her first-grade child. The child has a very good speaking vocabulary, but this is not reflected in her writing. She reads a little above grade level, but the parent feels the child "fakes it" by looking at the pictures and guessing based on the context of the story. The parent is concerned that the child is not reading so much as remembering what a book is about and filling in areas of

confusion with guesses. The parent points to the child's writing samples as further evidence. The day before, the child scripted:

My famble will go to the fare on Saturday we will ride the farus will. We will eat popzikls. I want to win a stuft aminul. (*My family will go to the fair on Saturday. We will ride the Ferris wheel. We will eat popsicles. I want to win a stuffed animal.*)

The teacher:
    a. Shares the parent's concern. They meet with the resource teacher to set up a program to address the problems.
    b. Advocates a wait-and-see policy. It is very early in the school year, and young children often demonstrate very rapid growth in previously problematic areas.
    c. Explains to the parent that the child is not experiencing problems. She is correctly using the sight words she has learned, applying her knowledge of word families to determine spelling of similar words, and correctly hearing phonemes and scripting the words that represent them. Her strong verbal vocabulary and her reading skills are further evidence she is doing well. Her writing will catch up as she learns further strategies and sight words.
    d. Explains to the parent that the child is not experiencing problems. She is eager to memorize sight words, and the teacher feels certain that the student's writing will radically improve as she memorizes the correct the spellings of all the words she wants to write.

85. Examples of onomatopoeia are:
    a. Sink, drink, mink, link.
    b. Their, there, they're.
    c. Drip, chirp, splash, giggle.
    d. *Think, in, thin, ink.*

86. "Code knowledge" facilitates reading fluency because:
    a. It brings the entirety of the student's previous experience to bear on decoding a text.
    b. It offers a framework for organizing new information by assigning code words to sets of ideas.
    c. There is no such thing as "code knowledge." The correct term is "core knowledge."
    d. It offers a systematic approach to untangling the wide variety of vowel sounds when an unfamiliar word is encountered.

87. The purpose of "targeted instruction" is to:
    a. Deliver instructions that are precise, clear, and direct so that students understand exactly what is expected.
    b. Accurately rank a group of learners from low achievers to high achievers so that the teacher knows from the beginning of the school year which students have less ability and will therefore need support.
    c. Teach students how to take information from a text and reorganize it into bulleted lists.
    d. Assess and target areas needing improvement as well as areas of greatest strength for each student to ensure that all members of a class are receiving instruction tailored to their specific needs.

88. Components of "explicit instruction" include:
   a. Clarifying the goal, modeling strategies, and offering explanations geared to a student's level of understanding.
   b. Determining the goal, offering strategies, and asking questions designed to ascertain whether understanding has been reached.
   c. Reassessing the goal, developing strategies, and determining whether further reassessing of the goal is required.
   d. Objectifying the goal, assessing strategies, and offering explanations geared toward a student's level of understanding.

89. A teacher has challenged a student with a book about Antarctica that is just beyond the high end of the student's Instructional level. The teacher points out that the student already knows quite a bit about penguins because the class studied them earlier in the year. He reminds the student that she's recently seen a television show about the seals that also live in Antarctic waters. The teacher gives the student a list of words she's likely to find in the text, and they discuss what those words might mean. The student begins to read, but stops to ask the teacher what *circumpolar* means. The teacher is also unfamiliar with the word, but reminds her that *circum* is a prefix. The student recalls that it means "about or around" and deduces that circumpolar most likely refers to something found around or in a polar region. This instructional approach is called:
   a. Modular instruction
   b. Scaffolding
   c. Linking
   d. Transmutation

90. The second graders are confused. They've learned to hear and count syllables. They understand that contractions such as *won't*, *didn't*, and *we're* represent two words converted into one. Now the teacher is trying to explain compound words. She has shown the children that a compound word is made of two words and has a meaning that is a little different from either of words that compose it. She pronounces *doghouse*, and asks if it is one word or two. "Two," the students correctly respond. The teacher now says *parent*. Again, the students tell her it's two words. The teacher explains there are two syllables but not two words. One child nods and says, "Like the word 'didn't.' That's two words but it sounds like one." What is the best way for the teacher to correct the students' misunderstanding?
   a. Point out compound words the children use throughout the day. Write them on the board, and ask students to list them in their writing journals.
   b. Assess the degree of confusion. Give the students a quiz listing a number of two-syllable words, compound words, and contractions. Ask the students to cross out the two-syllable words and contractions.
   c. Write a compound word such as doghouse on the board. Underline dog, and then house. Beneath the words draw a picture of a dog and a house, joined with a plus sign. Next, write another compound word and ask the class to draw the pictures in their journals. Give the students a handout with several compound words. Ask them to underline the two words, then to draw the pictures.
   d. Turn the lesson into fun by suggesting the students invent new compound words. Demonstrate by inventing one such as nosemitten instead of scarf. Children learn more readily when they are enjoying it.

91. An understanding of the meanings of prefixes and suffixes such as *dis, mis, un, re, able,* and *ment* are important for:
   a. Reading comprehension
   b. Word recognition
   c. Vocabulary building
   d. Reading fluency

92. VC, CVC, CCVC, CVCC, and CCVCC are among the types of:
   a. Homophones
   b. Closed syllables
   c. Monosyllabic words
   d. Polyglotal indicators

93. A student is taking a reading test. The teacher has blocked out a number of words. Each blank is assigned a set of three possible words. The student must select the correct word from each set so that the text makes sense. The student is taking:
   a. A cloze test
   b. A maze test
   c. A multiple-choice quiz
   d. A vocabulary test

94. When working with English Language Learners, the teacher should:
   a. Avoid idioms and slang, involve students in hands-on activities, reference students' prior knowledge, and speak slowly.
   b. Speak slowly, use monosyllabic words whenever possible, repeat each sentence three times before moving to the next sentence, and employ idioms but not slang.
   c. Use monosyllabic words whenever possible, repeat key instructions three times but not in a row, reference students' prior knowledge, and have students keep a journal of new vocabulary.
   d. Have students keep a journal of new vocabulary, reference students' prior knowledge, speak slowly, and involve students in hands-on activities.

95. Editing involves:
   a. Correcting surface features such as sentence fragments, spelling, and punctuation.
   b. Fine-tuning the underlying structure of the piece to make the theme stand out.
   c. Reconsidering ideas, adding or subtracting information, and changing the underlying structure.
   d. Adding illustrations, charts, and other useful addenda.

96. A seventh grader has never had much success with reading. Her ability to decode is rudimentary; she stops and starts when reading, frequently loses her place, or misreads an important word. She doesn't seem aware of where errors occur, or she does not attempt to correct them. When asked to tell about what she's read, her comprehension is minimal. To help her, instructional focus on which of the following would be most useful?
   a. Carefully organized lessons in decoding, sight words, vocabulary, and comprehension at least three to five times a week. These mini-lessons must be extremely clear, with the parts broken down to the lowest common denominator. The more tightly interwoven and systematized the instruction, the better chance this student will have.

b. A weekly lesson focusing on one aspect of reading. This student will be overwhelmed if too many strategies are offered at once. The instruction should focus first on recognizing sight words, then letter–sound association. Next, the girl needs an understanding of the rules of syntax.

c. The student isn't trying. Her instruction should be aimed at helping her learn to be self-motivated and disciplined in her approach to learning.

d. Comprehension strategies will help her grasp the overall meaning of a text. From there she can begin to drill down until she's able to combine various approaches that, working together, will enable her to read.

97. Silent reading fluency can best be assessed by:
   a. Having the student retell or summarize the material to determine how much was understood.
   b. Giving a written test that covers plot, theme, character development, sequence of events, rising action, climax, falling action, and outcome. A student must test at a 95% accuracy rate to be considered fluent at silent reading.
   c. Giving a three-minute Test of Silent Contextual Reading Fluency four times a year. The student is presented with text in which spaces between words and all punctuation have been removed. The student must divide one word from another with slash marks, as in the following example:
   The/little/sailboat/bobbed/so/far/in/the/distance/it/looked/like/a/toy. The more words a student accurately separates, the higher her silent reading fluency score.
   d. Silent reading fluency cannot be assessed. It is a private act between the reader and the text and does not invite critique.

98. A high school teacher has given her students an assignment to write a non-rhyming poem of three lines. The first and last lines each contain five syllables, and the middle line contains seven syllables. The students are writing a:
   a. Limerick
   b. Metaphor
   c. Villanelle
   d. Haiku

99. "Verbal dyspraxia" refers to:
   a. Trouble with the physical act of writing.
   b. Confusing word or sentence order while speaking.
   c. Misplacement of letters within words.
   d. An inability to process verbal information.

100. "Coarticulation" affects:
   a. Blending awareness
   b. Phonemic awareness

c. Sequencing
d. Aural awareness

Answer Explanations

1. The answer is a: Homophones. Homophones are a type of homonym that sound alike, but are spelled differently and have different meanings. Other examples are *two, to,* and *too; their, they're,* and *there.*

2. The answer is c: Argumentative essay. The goal of a persuasive essay is to convince the reader that the author's position or opinion on a controversial topic is correct. That opinion or position is called the argument. A persuasive essay argues a series of points, supported by facts and evidence.

3. The answer is d: Rate, accuracy, and prosody. Fluent readers are able to read smoothly and comfortably at a steady pace (rate). The more quickly a child reads, the greater the chance of leaving out a word or substituting one word for another (for example, *sink* instead of *shrink*). Fluent readers are able to maintain accuracy without sacrificing rate. Fluent readers also stress important words in a text, group words into rhythmic phrases, and read with intonation (prosody).

4. The answer is b: The number of unrecognizable words an English Language Learner encounters when reading a passage or listening to a teacher. Language load is one of the barriers English Language Learners face. To lighten this load, a teacher can rephrase, eliminate unnecessary words, divide complex sentences into smaller units, and teach essential vocabulary before the student begins the lesson.

5. The answer is a: A vowel. A syllable is a minimal sound unit arranged around a vowel. For example, *academic* has four syllables: *a/ca/dem/ic.* It is possible for a syllable to be a single vowel, as in the above example. It is not possible for a syllable to be a single consonant.

6. The answer is c: Fail, producing students at a Frustration reading level. Those reading below grade level are likely to give up entirely. Those reading at grade level are likely to get frustrated and form habits that will actually slow down their development. Giving students texts that are too far beyond their reach produces frustrated readers. In an effort to succeed, frustrated writers are likely to apply strategies that have worked for them in the past but cannot work in this case because the text is simply beyond them. Looking for contextual clues to understand the meaning of unfamiliar words requires that most of the words in the passage are familiar. Breaking unfamiliar words into individual phonemes or syllables can be effective, but not if the number of such words is excessive. In this case, students below reading level and students at reading level will become frustrated when the skills that have worked for them in the past now fail.

7. The answer is c: Tier-two words. Tier-two words are words that are used with high frequency across a variety of disciplines or words with multiple meanings. They are characteristic of mature language users. Knowing these words is crucial to attaining an acceptable level of reading comprehension and communication skills.

8. The answer is c: Reading at her Independent reading level. When reading independently, students are at the correct level if they read with at least 97% accuracy.

9. The answer is b: To correct an error in reading a student has made, specifically clarifying where and how the error was made so that the student can avoid similar errors in the future. A reading teacher offers corrective feedback to a student in order to explain why a particular error in reading is, in fact, an error. Corrective feedback is specific; it locates where and how the student went astray so that similar errors can be avoided in future reading.

10. The answer is c: Content-specific words. Because these words are specific to paleontology, it's unlikely the students know their meanings. Without understanding what these words mean, the students would not be able to understand the content of the passage they were about to read.

11. The answer is b: Prior knowledge is knowledge the student brings from previous life or learning experiences to the act of reading. It is not possible for a student to fully comprehend new knowledge without first integrating it with prior knowledge. Prior knowledge, which rises from experience and previous learning, provides a framework by which new knowledge gained from the act of reading can be integrated. Every act of reading enriches a student's well of prior knowledge and increases that student's future ability to comprehend more fully any new knowledge acquired through reading.

12. The answer is b: Understanding of context and vocabulary. In a cloze test, a reader is given a text with certain words blocked out. The reader must be able to determine probable missing words based on contextual clues. In order to supply these words, the reader must already know them.

13. The answer is a: Common words with irregular spelling. Sight words occur in many types of writing; they are high-frequency words. Sight words are also words with irregular spelling. Some examples of sight words include *talk, some,* and *the.* Fluent readers need to recognize these words visually.

14. The answer is d: Consonant digraph. A consonant digraph is group of consonants in which all letters represent a single sound.

15. The answer is a: Phonological awareness. Phonemic awareness is the ability to recognize sounds within words. Segmenting words and blending sounds are components of phonemic awareness. Phonological awareness includes an understanding of multiple components of spoken language. Ability to hear individual words within a vocalized stream and ability to identify spoken syllables are types of phonological awareness.

16. The answer is a: Letter–sound correspondence. Letter–sound correspondence relies on the relationship between a spoken sound or group of sounds and the letters conventionally used in English to write them.

17. The answer is a: Strategy instruction. Strategic instruction involves teaching a methodic approach to solving a reading problem. It consists of strategies done in steps which aid the reader in eliminating incorrect responses.

18. The answer is d: Familiar, frequently used words that do not need to be taught beyond primary grades. Common or basic words are the first tier of three-tier words. These words are widely used across the spoken and written spectrum. Some examples are *walk, go, wish, the, look, happy,* and *always.* This essential vocabulary is taught early in a reader's instruction, and beyond that it need not be taught.

19. The answer is b: The number of phonemes. A phoneme is the smallest measure of language sound. English language phonemes, about 40 in number, are composed of individual letters as well as letter combinations. A number of letters have more than one associated sound. For example, "c" can be pronounced as a hard "c" (cake) or a soft "c" (Cynthia). Vowels in particular have a number of possible pronunciations.

20. The answer is b: Consonant blend. Consonant blend refers to a group of consonants in which each letter represents a separate sound.

21. The answer is a: Fewer than 100 words in the time given. At the beginning of the school year, second-grade students should be able to read 50–80 words per minute. By the time they are well into the school year, second-grade-level reading is tracked at 85 words per minute.

22. The answer is d: None; sight words cannot be decoded. Readers must learn to recognize these words as wholes on sight. Sight words have irregular spelling. Segmenting them into syllables or using a phonemic approach are ineffective strategies to aid a reader in recognizing a sight word, because these approaches depend on rules a sight word doesn't follow. Word families group words that share common patterns of consonants and vowels. The spelling of those words is therefore regular, because they follow a predictable pattern. Sight words are irregular and do not follow a predictable pattern and must be instantaneously recognized for writing fluency. No decoding is useful.

23. The answer is d: A and B. English Language Learners are simultaneously learning to read in English and to apply patterns of intonation that are likely different from those of their first languages. While it's often useful to arrange reading time with a family member, in this particular case reading with a family member who is not a fluent English speaker may reinforce intonation patterns and pronunciation that are not correct. Therefore, C is not the answer. Both A and B afford English Language Learners the opportunity to become familiar with reading rates that are appropriate to the text and simultaneously expose them to prosody. They will not only see text, but will hear proper intonation patterns that are likely different than those of their first languages.

24. The answer is c: Alphabetic principle. The act of decoding involves first recognizing the sounds individual letters and letter groups make, and then blending the sounds to read the word. A child decoding the word *spin*, for example, would first pronounce *sp/i/n* as individual sound units. She then would repeat the sounds, smoothly blending them. Because decoding involves understanding letters and their sounds, it is sometimes known as the alphabetic principle.

25. The answer is c: Events. "Reading" a story's illustrations offers visual clues to characters and events in the proper order. A story's plot is what happens first, next, later, and finally.

26. The answer is a: Oral. Phonological awareness refers to an understanding of the sounds a word makes. While phonological awareness leads to fluent reading skills, activities designed to develop an awareness of word sounds are, by definition, oral.

27. The answer is b: Vocabulary. Strategizing in order to understand the meaning of a word, knowing multiple meanings of a single word, and applying background knowledge to glean a word's meaning are all ways in which an effective reader enhances vocabulary. Other skills include an awareness of word parts and word origins, the ability to apply word meanings in a variety of content areas, and a delight in learning the meanings of unfamiliar words.

28. The answer is c: She is reading at an Instructional level. In one minute, a student who misreads one or less than one word per twenty words, or with 95%–100% accuracy, is at an Independent reading level. A student who misreads one or less than one word per ten words, or with 90%–95% accuracy, is at an Instructional level. A student misreading more than one word out of ten, or with less than 90% accuracy, is at a Frustration level.

29. The answer is d: Decoding depends on an understanding of letter–sound relationships. As soon as a child understands enough letters and their correspondent sounds to read a few words, decoding should be introduced. The act of decoding involves first recognizing the sounds individual letters and letter groups in a word make and then blending the sounds to read the word. It's important to introduce the strategy as soon as a child knows enough letters and their corresponding sounds to read simple words.

30. The answer is c: Cause–effect words. Signal words give the reader hints about the purpose of a particular passage. Some signal words are concerned with comparing/contrasting, some with cause and effect, some with temporal sequencing, some with physical location, and some with a problem and its solution. The words *since, whether,* and *accordingly* are words used when describing an outcome. Outcomes have causes.

31. The answer is a: Outcome. Story action can be analyzed in terms of rising action, story climax, falling action, and resolution. Rising action consists of those events that occur before and lead up to the story's most dramatic moment, or climax. The climax occurs toward the end of the book, but rarely, if ever, right at the end. Following the climax, the consequences of that dramatic moment are termed falling action. The story reaches resolution with the outcome of the falling action.

32. The answer is c: Locate the vowels, then locate familiar word parts. Syllables are organized around vowels. In order to determine the syllables, this student should begin by locating the vowels. It's possible to have a syllable that is a single vowel (*a/gain*). It isn't possible to have a syllable that is a single consonant. Once the word has been broken into its component syllables the reader is able to study the syllables to find ones that are familiar and might give her a clue as to the word's meaning, such as certain prefixes or suffixes.

33. The answer is a: Nothing. These children are simply at an early stage in the reading/writing process. When emergent readers become aware of the connections between letters and sounds, and between reading and writing, they want to practice the skills they see proficient readers use. While a proficient writer knows that letters are

grouped into words and that words are constructed into sentences that move from left to right and from the top of the page to the bottom, an emergent reader/writer knows only that letters magically contain sounds that other people can read. It is necessary for children to pass through early stages in which they scribble-write and pretend they are scripting letters, which leads to a stage in which they actually do write the initial letter of a word all over the page. Next, the emergent reader/writer will write the initial letter of many of the words that belong in the sentence and will write them sequentially. KJM, for example, might mean *the cat chased a mouse.*

34. The answer is a: Scripting the end-sound to a word (KT=cat); leaving space between words; writing from the top left to the top right of the page, and from top to bottom. Each of these steps is progressively more abstract. Scripting the end-sound to a word helps a young writer recognize that words have beginnings and endings. This naturally leads to the willingness to separate words with white space so that they stand as individual entities. Once this step is reached, the child realizes that in English, writing progresses from left to right and from the top of the page to the bottom.

35. The answer is b: Ask the students to read their stories to her. Suggest they visit other children in the class and read to each of them. The teacher should encourage these students by "reading" what they have written, even if what she reads is incorrect. She might misread KJM as *Kathy jumped rope with Mandy.* Most children will not be upset by this, but will correct the teacher's misreading by reading what the letters really mean.

36. The answer is d: The teacher should encourage all students to "read" picture books from the first day of school. Talking about the pictures from page to page gives young readers the idea that books are arranged sequentially. Pictures also offer narrative coherence and contextual clues. Emergent readers who are encouraged to enjoy books will more readily embrace the act of reading. Holding a book and turning pages gives young readers a familiarity with them.

37. The answer is d: Students should be taught that writing is a process. By teaching students to apply spelling patterns found in common phonemic units, the spelling of many words can be deduced. Sight words that are high frequency and do not follow patterns found in other words (*the, guardian, colonel*) must be taught.

38. The answer is c: Identify and use groups of letters that occur in a word family. Analogizing is based on recognizing the pattern of letters in words that share sound similarities. If the pattern is found at the end of a family of words, it is called a *rhyme.* Some examples of rhyme are *rent, sent, bent,* and *dent.* If the pattern is found at the beginning of the family of words, it is frequently a consonant *blend* such as *street, stripe,* or *strong,* in which all the letters are pronounced, or the pattern is a consonant digraph, in which the letters are taken together to represent a single sound such as in *phone, phonics,* or *phantom.*

39. The answer is a: Useful. The child will feel more confident because the story is already familiar. She will also feel that the lesson is a conversation of sorts, and that she is communicating successfully. She will be motivated to learn the English words because they are meaningful and highly charged. As a newly arrived immigrant, the child feels overwhelmed. Presenting her with a book of folk tales from her country tells her that she needn't lose her culture in order to function in this one. It also comforts her by reminding

her that her past and present are linked. Allowing her to speak in Korean helps her express herself without fear of judgment or failure. Presenting her with an English vocabulary that is meaningful ensures that she will eagerly embrace these words, her first words in her new language.

40. The answer is d: Cultural load. Cultural load is concerned with how the relationship between language and culture can help or hinder learning. By using the Korean folk tale, the teacher offered the child the opportunity to learn new words in a context that was culturally familiar. By demonstrating respect for her student's culture, she helped lighten the cultural load.

41. The answer is c: Right and left; left. Researchers have discovered through brain imaging that a dyslexic reader uses both sides of the brain. Non-dyslexic readers use only the left side.

42. The answer is b: Revising. Revision (literally, re+vision) is the act of "seeing again." When revising, writers examine what they have written in order to improve the meaning of the work. Fine-tuning word choices, moving information to another location, and adding or deleting words are all acts of revision.

43. The answer is d: Prefixes, appearing at the beginning of base words to change their meanings. Suffixes appear at the end of words. Prefixes are attached to the beginning of words to change their meanings. *Un+happy, bi+monthly,* and *re+examine* are prefixes that, by definition, change the meanings of the words to which they are attached.

44. The answer is d: Dog, sit, leg. CVC words are composed of a consonant, a vowel, and a consonant. To learn to read them, students must be familiar with the letters used and their sounds. A teacher can present a word like *sit* to students who also know the consonants *b/f/h/p* and ask them to create a word family of other CVC words. The students will be able to read *bit, fit, hit,* and *pit* because they are similar to the word *sit* they have just learned.

45. The answer is c: Context. By considering the other words in the story, the student can determine the missing words. The student is depending on the information supplied by the rest of the story. This information puts the story into context.

46. The answer is d: All of the above. Metacognition means a reader's awareness of her own reading processes as she improves reading comprehension. Other elements of metacognition include awareness of areas in the text where the reader fails to comprehend and an understanding of how the text is structured.

47. The answer is a: Cooperative learning and reading comprehension. Cooperative learning occurs when a group of students at various levels of reading ability have goals in common. Reading comprehension is achieved through reading both orally and silently, developing vocabulary, a reader's ability to predict what will occur in a piece of writing, a reader's ability to summarize the main points in a piece of writing, and a reader's ability to reflect on the text's meaning and connect that meaning to another text or personal experience.

48. The answer is b: Understanding the meaning of words that are not familiar. Context cues offer insight into the probable meaning of unfamiliar words.

49. The answer is c: Observe the child over the course of a week or two. Draw her into conversation and determine if her vocabulary is limited, if she displays emotional problems, or if her reticence could have another cause. Note how the child interacts with others in the class. Does she ever initiate conversation? If another child initiates, does she respond? Until the teacher monitors the child's verbal abilities and habits, she cannot determine if the lack of interaction suggests a learning disability, an emotional problem, or simply a shy personality. The teacher should informally observe the child over a period of time, noting if and when she initiates or responds to oral language, if she is reading with apparent comprehension, if her vocabulary is limited, and the degree to which the child is interested in understanding.

50. The answer is b: Intervention. She can identify groups of letters, but is not able to apply letter–sound association. By first grade, a child should understand how to use word families to decode words. It is good that she can recognize the rhymes (common letter groups at the end of a word), but the fact that she does not know sounds associated with the letters that begin the word is troubling. She needs focused help on strengthening her ability to identify words.

51. The answer is c: Persuasive. The author is hoping to persuade or convince readers to avoid alcohol and tobacco by providing them with facts as well as by using rhetorical devices such as dispelling opposing arguments.

52. The answer is c: They meet to discuss areas the teacher is most concerned about and decide on the teacher's goals. In order to best achieve goals, those goals must be understood and established.

53. The answer is d: Being able to identify rhyme is an important element of phonological awareness. Young children use language in a solely oral way. Oral language is composed of separate sounds that are represented in written form by the alphabet. In order to read, a child must first have a sense of the sounds that are used in English (phonological awareness). By helping children hear the difference between rhyming and non-rhyming words, the teacher is preparing them to make the transition to sound–letter association and word families.

54. The answer is a: Closed, open, silent *e*, vowel team, vowel-*r*, and consonant-*le*. A closed syllable ends with a consonant, such as *cat*. Open syllables end with a vowel, such as *he*. Vowel team syllables contain two vowels working together, such as *main*. Vowel-*r* syllables such as *er* and *or* frequently occur as suffixes. Consonant-*le* syllables also typically occur as suffixes, such as *battle* or *terrible*.

55. The answer is a: Strategies to increase comprehension and to build vocabulary. The student should receive instruction focused on just those areas in which he is exhibiting difficulty. Improved vocabulary will give him greater skill at comprehending the meaning of a particular text. Strategies focused on enhancing comprehension together with a stronger vocabulary will provide the greatest help.

56. The answer is b: Through a combination of standardized testing, informal teacher observations, attention to grades, objective-linked assessments, and systematized charting of data over time. Reading comprehension and vocabulary cannot be sufficiently assessed with occasional, brief studies. Continuous observation, high-stakes and standardized testing, attention to grades, and closely tracking the outcomes of objective-linked assessments are interrelated tools that, when systematically organized, offer a thorough understanding of students' strengths and weaknesses.

57. The answer is a: An Oral Reading Fluency assessment. ORF stands for oral reading fluency. This assessment measures the words correct per minute (WCPM) by subtracting the number of errors made from the total number of words orally read in a one- to two-minute period of time. It is used to find a student's Instructional reading level, to identify readers who are having difficulties, and to track developing fluency and word recognition over time.

58. The answer is a: At the end of the year, to determine if instructional goals established at the beginning of the year have been successfully reached. An outcome assessment given at the end of the year helps the reading teacher determine which students have reached instructional goals and do not need further support and which students will benefit from continued support.

59. The answer is d: Especially important to English Language Learners and students with reading disabilities. Word recognition is required for reading fluency and is important to all readers, but it is especially so to English Language Learners and students with reading disabilities. It can be effectively taught through precisely calibrated word study instruction designed to provide readers with reading and writing strategies for successful word analysis.

60. The answer is a: Proficiency with oral language enhances students' phonemic awareness and increases vocabulary. Understanding that words are scripted with specific letters representing specific sounds is essential to decoding a text. Students cannot effectively learn to read without the ability to decode. An enhanced vocabulary supports the act of reading; the larger an emergent reader's vocabulary, the more quickly he will learn to read. He will be able to decode more words, which he can organize into word families, which he can use to decode unfamiliar words.

61. The answer is c. Read the documents quickly, looking for key words in order to gather the basic premise of each. Skimming allows a reader to quickly gain a broad understanding of a piece of writing in order to determine if a more thorough reading is warranted. Skimming allows students who are researching a topic on the Internet or in print to consider a substantial body of information in order to select only that of particular relevance.

62. The answer is b. Expository. Expository essays clarify an idea, explain an event, or interpret facts. The position the author takes is often supported with statistics, quotations, or other evidence researched from a variety of sources.

63. The answer is b: Persuasive. A persuasive essay takes a strong position about a controversial topic and offers factual evidence to support this position. The goal of a

persuasive paper is to convince the audience that the claim is true based on the evidence provided.

64. The answer is a: However, the myth of "safe cigarettes," questions about nicotine addiction, and denials about the dangers of secondhand smoke have proven to be propaganda and lies. A thesis statement offers a hypothesis or opinion that the remainder of the paper then sets out to prove. Oftentimes, the thesis statement also offers a clear road map of the paper, foreshadowing the focuses of the paragraphs that follow and the order in which they will appear.

65. The answer is d. The myth of "safe cigarettes," questions about nicotine addiction, and the dangers of secondhand smoke. These three foci are presented in the thesis statement in this order and will be fleshed out in the following three paragraphs as the body of the essay.

66. The answer is c. Example. Example essays, also called illustration essays, are simple, straightforward pieces that depend on clearly described examples to make their points. An example essay isn't trying to convince the reader (argumentative), compare similar or dissimilar things (compare/contrast), or point to relationships such as cause and effect. Often, example essays teach the reader how to accomplish something or about something.

67. The answer is c: Are homophones. Homophones are words that are pronounced the same, but differ in meaning. For example, a bride wears a 2 caret ring, but a horse eats a carrot.

68. The answer is a: Collaborative learning. A group of students working together on a project are applying numerous learning strategies at once. Collaborative learning is a hands-on approach that actively involves students in the learning process. Students involved in collaborative learning typically retain the lesson better.

69. The answer is c: Biography. A biography relates information about part of the life of an individual. An autobiography is a biography about the writer's own life. A memoir is also autobiographical, but focuses on a theme. Historical fiction uses a setting or event based in historical fact as the background for characters and/or action that is invented.

70. The answer is c: Students will do online research about the cultural, economic, or political events that were occurring during the specific time about which they've written. By researching the historic setting that cradled the events their interviewee discussed, students are simultaneously broadening their understanding of the context and working in a different content area.

71. The answer is b. Brainstorming and a compare/contrast strategy. Brainstorming is a prewriting activity in which an individual or group responds to a specific question by considering any and all responses that arise without editing, prioritizing, or selecting. Once the brainstorming session is complete, students look at the results and eliminate any responses that are not useful, then group and prioritize the remaining responses. In this example, the students are having a collaborative learning experience in that they are brainstorming together; however, collaborative learning is not a strategy per se, but is the outcome of a strategy. The students are also employing a compare/contrast strategy in that

they are looking both at how the two writing styles share common elements and how they are distinct.

72. The answer is c. Writing styles. Both Anderson and the Grimms wrote in the same genre, that of fairy tales. Genre refers to types of writing. Mystery, romance, adventure, historical fiction, and fairy tales are some examples of genres. A genre can include many different authors and writing styles. These students are being asked to compare two distinct writing styles within a single genre in order to locate similarities and differences.

73. The answer is b. Comprehension. This exercise requires students to examine the authors' use of setting, plot, pacing, word choice, syntactical structures, narration, mood, metaphors, point of view, voice, and character development to find ways in which they are similar as well as different. In so doing, the students are discovering that language shapes meaning in ways both subtle and profound.

74. The answer is c: The importance of culture to meaning. Authors make thousands of decisions in the act of writing. What point of view to take, how much weight to give an event, what to reveal about a character, and what words will most effectively express the writer's intention are but a few of these decisions. While many of these decisions are consciously artistic choices, many are unconscious and imbedded in the cultural expectations of time and place in which the author has lived. To understand a text to the fullest degree possible, it is necessary to read it with an eye to the cultural framework from whence it came.

75. The answer is a: Give each child a piece of drawing paper that has been folded in half and then again, creating four boxes, along with a piece that has not been folded. The teacher should then ask the students to draw a cartoon about the story. Each of the first four boxes will show the events in order. The second page is to show how the story ends. When a child is able to visually see the way a familiar story has unfolded, that child can find causal or thematic connections in the action that increases her comprehension of the story overall. Asking the class to draw a single picture or to draw the beginning and end doesn't sufficiently demonstrate the importance of order to meaning. While some first graders may be able to create their own cartoon stories that demonstrate a logical series of events, many first graders are not yet ready to organize thought into a linear progression.

76. The answer is a: Sonnet. There are three primary types of sonnets. The Shakespearean sonnet is specifically what these students are reading. A Spenserian sonnet is also composed of three four-line stanzas followed by a two-line couplet; however, the rhymes are not contained within each stanza but spill from one stanza to the next (*abab bcbc cdcd ee*). A Petrarchan sonnet divides into an eight-line stanza and a six-line stanza.

77. The answer is d: Compare and contrast. Asking children to write a list provides them with a visual model that is a side-by-side comparison of the two countries. In creating that visual model, each student first has to organize his or her thoughts mentally, deciding whether each particular item under consideration shares more or less in common with the other.

78. The answer is c: *People celebrate marriages, births, and historical events.* The overlapping area is reserved for those items that are not culturally specific but are seen in both cultures.

79. The answer is d. A Venn diagram. A Venn diagram uses two or more circles with a common, overlapping area as a model to organize similar and dissimilar elements. The greater the number of similarities, the closer the circles must be and consequently, the greater the overlapping area. The fewer the number of similarities, the farther apart the circles will be and, consequently, the smaller the overlapping area.

80. The answer is a. Dysgraphia. Dysgraphic individuals have difficulty with the physical act of writing. They find holding and manipulating a pencil problematic. Their letters are primitively formed, and their handwriting is illegible.

81. The answer is b. Cliché. While "Pretty as a picture" is a simile (comparison of two unlike things using *like* or *as*), its overuse has turned it into a cliché. A cliché is a trite platitude.

82. The answer is b. Vocabulary. The tightly controlled syllabic requirements will cause students to search for words outside their normal vocabularies that will fit the rigid framework and still express the writer's intended meanings. Often, students will rediscover a word whose meaning they know, but they don't often use.

83. The answer is c. Brainstorming a list of verbs that mean ways of talking or ways of going, then adding them to the word wall along with some nouns that specify common topics. Second graders aren't developmentally ready for a thesaurus; most will believe that any words in a particular list are interchangeable. For example, a student who wrote *My little sister walks like a baby* might find the verbs *strut, sidle,* and *amble* in the thesaurus. None of these verbs would be an appropriate substitution. Supplementing a noun with an adjective often results in flat writing: *There's a tree in my yard* might become *There's a nice tree in my big yard.* Adjectives such as *pretty, fun, cute, funny,* and so forth don't add much in terms of meaning, but they are the adjectives younger writers reach for first. A more specific noun is both more meaningful and more interesting. *There's a weeping willow in my yard* is evocative.

84. The correct answer is c: Explains to the parent that the child is not experiencing problems. She is correctly using the sight words she has learned, applying her knowledge of word families to determine spelling of similar words, and correctly hearing phonemes and scripting the words that represent them. Her strong verbal vocabulary and her reading skills are further evidence she is doing well. Her writing will catch up as she learns further strategies and sight words.

85. The answer is c: *Drip, chirp, splash, giggle.* Onomatopoeia refers to words that sound like what they represent.

86. The answer is d: It offers a systematic approach to untangling the wide variety of vowel sounds when an unfamiliar word is encountered. Code knowledge, also called orthographic tendencies, is a helpful approach to decoding a word when multiple pronunciation possibilities exist. For example, in the words *toe, go, though,* and *low,* the long O sound is written in a variety of ways. A code knowledge approach teaches a reader to first try a short

vowel sound. If that doesn't help, the reader should consider the different ways the vowel or vowel groups can be pronounced, based on what he knows about other words.

87. The answer is d: Assess and target areas needing improvement as well as areas of greatest strength for each student to ensure the all members of a class are receiving instruction tailored to their specific needs.

88. The answer is a: Clarifying the goal, modeling strategies, and offering explanations geared to a student's level of understanding. Explicit instruction is well organized and structured, and it offers easily understood steps and depends in part on frequent reference to previously learned materials.

89. The answer is b: Scaffolding. Using this strategic approach, a teacher assigns a task that is just beyond the student's current level. The teacher encourages the student's attempts at comprehension by offering various supports that largely depend on prior knowledge, in order to develop the student's willingness to move forward into uncharted territory as a confident independent learner.

90. The answer is c: Write a compound word such as *doghouse* on the board. Underline *dog,* and then *house.* Beneath the words draw a picture of a dog and a house, joined with a plus sign. Next, write another compound word and ask the class to draw the pictures in their journals. Give the students a handout with several compound words. Ask them to underline the two words, then to draw the pictures. Students will discover that compound words are composed of two distinct words that in combination mean something new but related.

91. The answer is a. Reading comprehension. Prefixes and suffixes change the meanings of the root word to which they are attached. A student who understands that *un* means "not" will be able to decipher the meanings of words such as *unwanted, unhappy,* or *unreasonable.*

92. The answer is b: Closed syllables. Closed syllables are those that end with a consonant. *At, dog, spit, duck,* and *pluck* are all examples of closed syllables.

93. The answer is b: A maze test. A maze test is a specific type of cloze test. In a cloze test, words are deleted and the reader must supply the missing words using contextual clues and vocabulary that is familiar. A maze test is a multiple-choice application of a cloze test.

94. The answer is a: Avoid idioms and slang, involve students in hands-on activities, reference students' prior knowledge, and speak slowly. Teachers of English Language Learners should not employ idioms and slang in their instruction because these informal uses of speech are likely to confuse the students. Involving students in hands-on activities such as group reading and language play makes the experience both more meaningful and more immediate. New knowledge can only be absorbed by attaching it to prior knowledge, referencing what students already know is essential. Speaking slowly to English Language Learners is important, because they are processing what is being said at a slower rate than a native speaker.

95. The answer is a: Correcting surface features such as sentence fragments, spelling, and punctuation. Editing is the final step in the writing process. The writer has already decided the ideas or events are in proper order, have been sufficiently described, and are clear. Now

the writer turns her attention to surface features, "scrubbing" errors in spelling, punctuation, and syntax from the writing.

96. The answer is a: Carefully organized lessons in decoding, sight words, vocabulary, and comprehension at least three to five times a week. These mini-lessons must be extremely clear, with the parts broken down to the lowest common denominator. The more tightly interwoven and systematized the instruction, the better chance this student will have. This type of learner needs, first and foremost, instruction that has been highly organized into a system that will make sense to her. If possible, she should receive private instruction on a daily basis. The instruction needs to focus on decoding, recognizing words, reading with increasing fluency, enhancing vocabulary, and comprehension. She should be working at the Instructional level, or with texts she can read with at least 90% accuracy.

97. The answer is c: Giving a three-minute Test of Silent Contextual Reading Fluency four times a year. The student is presented with text in which spaces between words and all punctuation have been removed. The student must divide one word from another with slash marks, as in the following example:
The/little/sailboat/bobbed/so/far/in/the/distance/it/looked/like/a/toy. The more words a student accurately separates, then the higher her silent reading fluency score. Silent reading fluency can be monitored over time by giving the Test of Silent Contextual Reading Fluency (TSCRF) four times a year. A similar assessment tool is the Test of Silent Word Reading Fluency (TOSWRF), in which words of increasing complexity are given as a single, undifferentiated, and unpunctuated strand. As with the TSCRF, three minutes are given for the student to separate each word from the next.
Itwillcannotschoolbecomeagendaconsistentphilosophysuperfluous is an example of such a strand.

98. The answer is d. Haiku. Based on a Japanese form of poetry, haiku have become popular with students and teachers alike. Reading and writing haiku helps younger students become aware of syllables and helps older students learn about subtleties of vocabulary.

99. The answer is b. Confusing word or sentence order while speaking. Dyspraxic individuals do not process spoken language sequentially due to a neurological distortion. The dislocation of sounds within a word, such as vocalizing *lamp* instead of *palm*, is one indication of verbal dyspraxia.

100. The answer is b: Phonemic awareness. Vocalizing words involves arranging a series of continuous, voice, unvoiced, and stop sounds. As one sound is being uttered, the tongue and lips are already assuming the shape required by the next sound in the word. This process, which is not conscious, can distort individual sounds. One sound can slur into another, clip the end of the previous sound, or flatten or heighten a sound. For children who have difficulty hearing distinct phonemic sounds, individual instruction may be required.

Secret Key #1 - Time is Your Greatest Enemy

Pace Yourself

Wear a watch. At the beginning of the test, check the time (or start a chronometer on your watch to count the minutes), and check the time after every few questions to make sure you are "on schedule."

If you are forced to speed up, do it efficiently. Usually one or more answer choices can be eliminated without too much difficulty. Above all, don't panic. Don't speed up and just begin guessing at random choices. By pacing yourself, and continually monitoring your progress against your watch, you will always know exactly how far ahead or behind you are with your available time. If you find that you are one minute behind on the test, don't skip one question without spending any time on it, just to catch back up. Take 15 fewer seconds on the next four questions, and after four questions you'll have caught back up. Once you catch back up, you can continue working each problem at your normal pace.

Furthermore, don't dwell on the problems that you were rushed on. If a problem was taking up too much time and you made a hurried guess, it must be difficult. The difficult questions are the ones you are most likely to miss anyway, so it isn't a big loss. It is better to end with more time than you need than to run out of time.

Lastly, sometimes it is beneficial to slow down if you are constantly getting ahead of time. You are always more likely to catch a careless mistake by working more slowly than quickly, and among very high-scoring test takers (those who are likely to have lots of time left over), careless errors affect the score more than mastery of material.

Secret Key #2 - Guessing is not Guesswork

You probably know that guessing is a good idea - unlike other standardized tests, there is no penalty for getting a wrong answer. Even if you have no idea about a question, you still have a 20-25% chance of getting it right.

Most test takers do not understand the impact that proper guessing can have on their score. Unless you score extremely high, guessing will significantly contribute to your final score.

Monkeys Take the Test

What most test takers don't realize is that to insure that 20-25% chance, you have to guess randomly. If you put 20 monkeys in a room to take this test, assuming they answered once per question and behaved themselves, on average they would get 20-25% of the questions correct. Put 20 test takers in the room, and the average will be much lower among guessed questions. Why?

1. The test writers intentionally writes deceptive answer choices that "look" right. A test taker has no idea about a question, so picks the "best looking" answer, which is often wrong. The monkey has no idea what looks good and what doesn't, so will consistently be lucky about 20-25% of the time.
2. Test takers will eliminate answer choices from the guessing pool based on a hunch or intuition. Simple but correct answers often get excluded, leaving a 0% chance of being correct. The monkey has no clue, and often gets lucky with the best choice.

This is why the process of elimination endorsed by most test courses is flawed and detrimental to your performance- test takers don't guess, they make an ignorant stab in the dark that is usually worse than random.

$5 Challenge

Let me introduce one of the most valuable ideas of this course- the $5 challenge:

You only mark your "best guess" if you are willing to bet $5 on it.
You only eliminate choices from guessing if you are willing to bet $5 on it.

Why $5? Five dollars is an amount of money that is small yet not insignificant, and can really add up fast (20 questions could cost you $100). Likewise, each answer choice on one question of the test will have a small impact on your overall score, but it can really add up to a lot of points in the end.

The process of elimination IS valuable.

However, if you accidentally eliminate the right answer or go on a hunch for an incorrect answer, your chances drop dramatically: to 0%. By guessing among all the answer choices, you are GUARANTEED to have a shot at the right answer.

That's why the $5 test is so valuable- if you give up the advantage and safety of a pure guess, it had better be worth the risk.

What we still haven't covered is how to be sure that whatever guess you make is truly random. Here's the easiest way:

Always pick the first answer choice among those remaining.
Such a technique means that you have decided, **before you see a single test question**, exactly how you are going to guess- and since the order of choices tells you nothing about which one is correct, this guessing technique is perfectly random.

This section is not meant to scare you away from making educated guesses or eliminating choices- you just need to define when a choice is worth eliminating. The $5 test, along with a pre-defined random guessing strategy, is the best way to make sure you reap all of the benefits of guessing.

Secret Key #3 - Practice Smarter, Not Harder

Many test takers delay the test preparation process because they dread the awful amounts of practice time they think necessary to succeed on the test. We have refined an effective method that will take you only a fraction of the time.

There are a number of "obstacles" in your way to succeed. Among these are answering questions, finishing in time, and mastering test-taking strategies. All must be executed on the day of the test at peak performance, or your score will suffer. The test is a mental marathon that has a large impact on your future.

Just like a marathon runner, it is important to work your way up to the full challenge. So first you just worry about questions, and then time, and finally strategy:

Success Strategy

1. Find a good source for practice tests.
2. If you are willing to make a larger time investment, consider using more than one study guide- often the different approaches of multiple authors will help you "get" difficult concepts.
3. Take a practice test with no time constraints, with all study helps "open book." Take your time with questions and focus on applying strategies.
4. Take a practice test with time constraints, with all guides "open book."
5. Take a final practice test with no open material and time limits

If you have time to take more practice tests, just repeat step 5. By gradually exposing yourself to the full rigors of the test environment, you will condition your mind to the stress of test day and maximize your success.

Secret Key #4 - Prepare, Don't Procrastinate

Let me state an obvious fact: if you take the test three times, you will get three different scores. This is due to the way you feel on test day, the level of preparedness you have, and, despite the test writers' claims to the contrary, some tests WILL be easier for you than others.

Since your future depends so much on your score, you should maximize your chances of success. In order to maximize the likelihood of success, you've got to prepare in advance. This means taking practice tests and spending time learning the information and test taking strategies you will need to succeed.

Never take the test as a "practice" test, expecting that you can just take it again if you need to. Feel free to take sample tests on your own, but when you go to take the official test, be prepared, be focused, and do your best the first time!

Secret Key #5 - Test Yourself

Everyone knows that time is money. There is no need to spend too much of your time or too little of your time preparing for the test. You should only spend as much of your precious time preparing as is necessary for you to get the score you need.

Once you have taken a practice test under real conditions of time constraints, then you will know if you are ready for the test or not.

If you have scored extremely high the first time that you take the practice test, then there is not much point in spending countless hours studying. You are already there.

Benchmark your abilities by retaking practice tests and seeing how much you have improved. Once you score high enough to guarantee success, then you are ready.

If you have scored well below where you need, then knuckle down and begin studying in earnest. Check your improvement regularly through the use of practice tests under real conditions. Above all, don't worry, panic, or give up. The key is perseverance!

Then, when you go to take the test, remain confident and remember how well you did on the practice tests. If you can score high enough on a practice test, then you can do the same on the real thing.

General Strategies

The most important thing you can do is to ignore your fears and jump into the test immediately- do not be overwhelmed by any strange-sounding terms. You have to jump into the test like jumping into a pool- all at once is the easiest way.

Make Predictions

As you read and understand the question, try to guess what the answer will be. Remember that several of the answer choices are wrong, and once you begin reading them, your mind will immediately become cluttered with answer choices designed to throw you off. Your mind is typically the most focused immediately after you have read the question and digested its contents. If you can, try to predict what the correct answer will be. You may be surprised at what you can predict.

Quickly scan the choices and see if your prediction is in the listed answer choices. If it is, then you can be quite confident that you have the right answer. It still won't hurt to check the other answer choices, but most of the time, you've got it!

Answer the Question

It may seem obvious to only pick answer choices that answer the question, but the test writers can create some excellent answer choices that are wrong. Don't pick an answer just because it sounds right, or you believe it to be true. It MUST answer the question. Once you've made your selection, always go back and check it against the question and make sure that you didn't misread the question, and the answer choice does answer the question posed.

Benchmark

After you read the first answer choice, decide if you think it sounds correct or not. If it doesn't, move on to the next answer choice. If it does, mentally mark that answer choice. This doesn't mean that you've definitely selected it as your answer choice, it just means that it's the best you've seen thus far. Go ahead and read the next choice. If the next choice is worse than the one you've already selected, keep going to the next answer choice. If the next choice is better than the choice you've already selected, mentally mark the new answer choice as your best guess.

The first answer choice that you select becomes your standard. Every other answer choice must be benchmarked against that standard. That choice is correct until proven otherwise by another answer choice beating it out. Once you've decided that no other answer choice seems as good, do one final check to ensure that your answer choice answers the question posed.

Valid Information

Don't discount any of the information provided in the question. Every piece of information may be necessary to determine the correct answer. None of the information in the question is there to throw you off (while the answer choices will certainly have information to throw you off). If two seemingly unrelated topics are discussed, don't ignore either. You can be confident there is a relationship, or it wouldn't be included in the question, and you are probably going to have to determine what is that relationship to find the answer.

Avoid "Fact Traps"

Don't get distracted by a choice that is factually true. Your search is for the answer that answers the question. Stay focused and don't fall for an answer that is true but incorrect. Always go back to the question and make sure you're choosing an answer that actually answers the question and is not just a true statement. An answer can be factually correct, but it MUST answer the question asked. Additionally, two answers can both be seemingly correct, so be sure to read all of the answer choices, and make sure that you get the one that BEST answers the question.

Milk the Question

Some of the questions may throw you completely off. They might deal with a subject you have not been exposed to, or one that you haven't reviewed in years. While your lack of knowledge about the subject will be a hindrance, the question itself can give you many clues that will help you find the correct answer. Read the question carefully and look for clues. Watch particularly for adjectives and nouns describing difficult terms or words that you don't recognize. Regardless of if you completely understand a word or not, replacing it with a synonym either provided or one you more familiar with may help you to understand what the questions are asking. Rather than wracking your mind about specific detailed information concerning a difficult term or word, try to use mental substitutes that are easier to understand.

The Trap of Familiarity

Don't just choose a word because you recognize it. On difficult questions, you may not recognize a number of words in the answer choices. The test writers don't put "make-believe" words on the test; so don't think that just because you only recognize all the words in one answer choice means that answer choice must be correct. If you only recognize words in one answer choice, then focus on that one. Is it correct? Try your best to determine if it is correct. If it is, that is great, but if it doesn't, eliminate it. Each word and answer choice you eliminate increases your chances of getting the question correct, even if you then have to guess among the unfamiliar choices.

Eliminate Answers

Eliminate choices as soon as you realize they are wrong. But be careful! Make sure you consider all of the possible answer choices. Just because one appears right, doesn't mean that the next one won't be even better! The test writers will usually put more than one good answer choice for every question, so read all of them. Don't worry if you are stuck between two that seem right. By getting down to just two remaining possible choices, your odds are now 50/50. Rather than wasting too much time, play the odds. You are guessing, but guessing wisely, because you've been able to knock out some of the answer choices that you know are wrong. If you are eliminating choices and realize that the last answer choice you are left with is also obviously wrong, don't panic. Start over and consider each choice again. There may easily be something that you missed the first time and will realize on the second pass.

Tough Questions

If you are stumped on a problem or it appears too hard or too difficult, don't waste time. Move on! Remember though, if you can quickly check for obviously incorrect answer choices, your chances of guessing correctly are greatly improved. Before you completely give up, at least try to knock out a couple of possible answers. Eliminate what you can and then guess at the remaining answer choices before moving on.

Brainstorm

If you get stuck on a difficult question, spend a few seconds quickly brainstorming. Run through the complete list of possible answer choices. Look at each choice and ask yourself, "Could this answer the question satisfactorily?" Go through each answer choice and consider it independently of the other. By systematically going through all possibilities, you may find something that you would otherwise overlook. Remember that when you get stuck, it's important to try to keep moving.

Read Carefully

Understand the problem. Read the question and answer choices carefully. Don't miss the question because you misread the terms. You have plenty of time to read each question thoroughly and make sure you understand what is being asked. Yet a happy medium must be attained, so don't waste too much time. You must read carefully, but efficiently.

Face Value

When in doubt, use common sense. Always accept the situation in the problem at face value. Don't read too much into it. These problems will not require you to make huge leaps of logic. The test writers aren't trying to throw you off with a cheap trick. If you have to go beyond creativity and make a leap of logic in order to have an answer choice answer the question, then you should look at the other answer choices. Don't overcomplicate the problem by creating theoretical relationships or explanations that will warp time or space. These are normal problems rooted in reality. It's just that the applicable relationship or explanation may not be readily apparent and you have to figure things out. Use your common sense to interpret anything that isn't clear.

Prefixes

If you're having trouble with a word in the question or answer choices, try dissecting it. Take advantage of every clue that the word might include. Prefixes and suffixes can be a huge help. Usually they allow you to determine a basic meaning. Pre- means before, post- means after, pro - is positive, de- is negative. From these prefixes and suffixes, you can get an idea of the general meaning of the word and try to put it into context. Beware though of any traps. Just because con is the opposite of pro, doesn't necessarily mean congress is the opposite of progress!

Hedge Phrases

Watch out for critical "hedge" phrases, such as likely, may, can, will often, sometimes, often, almost, mostly, usually, generally, rarely, sometimes. Question writers insert these hedge phrases to cover every possibility. Often an answer choice will be wrong simply because it leaves no room for exception. Avoid answer choices that have definitive words like "exactly," and "always".

Switchback Words

Stay alert for "switchbacks". These are the words and phrases frequently used to alert you to shifts in thought. The most common switchback word is "but". Others include although, however, nevertheless, on the other hand, even though, while, in spite of, despite, regardless of.

New Information

Correct answer choices will rarely have completely new information included. Answer choices typically are straightforward reflections of the material asked about and will directly relate to the question. If a new piece of information is included in an answer choice that doesn't even seem to relate to the topic being asked about, then that answer choice is likely incorrect. All of the information needed to answer the question is usually provided for you, and so you should not have to make guesses that are unsupported or choose answer choices that require unknown information that cannot be reasoned on its own.

Time Management

On technical questions, don't get lost on the technical terms. Don't spend too much time on any one question. If you don't know what a term means, then since you don't have a dictionary, odds are you aren't going to get much further. You should immediately recognize terms as whether or not you know them. If you don't, work with the other clues that you have, the other answer choices and terms provided, but don't waste too much time trying to figure out a difficult term.

Contextual Clues

Look for contextual clues. An answer can be right but not correct. The contextual clues will help you find the answer that is most right and is correct. Understand the context in which a phrase or statement is made. This will help you make important distinctions.

Don't Panic

Panicking will not answer any questions for you. Therefore, it isn't helpful. When you first see the question, if your mind goes blank, take a deep breath. Force yourself to mechanically go through the steps of solving the problem and using the strategies you've learned.

Pace Yourself

Don't get clock fever. It's easy to be overwhelmed when you're looking at a page full of questions, your mind is full of random thoughts and feeling confused, and the clock is ticking down faster than you would like. Calm down and maintain the pace that you have set for yourself. As long as you are on track by monitoring your pace, you are guaranteed to have enough time for yourself. When you get to the last few minutes of the test, it may seem like you won't have enough time left, but if you only have as many questions as you should have left at that point, then you're right on track!

Answer Selection

The best way to pick an answer choice is to eliminate all of those that are wrong, until only one is left and confirm that is the correct answer. Sometimes though, an answer choice may immediately look right. Be careful! Take a second to make sure that the other choices are not equally obvious. Don't make a hasty mistake. There are only two times that you should stop before checking other answers. First is when you are positive that the answer choice you have selected is correct. Second is when time is almost out and you have to make a quick guess!

Check Your Work

Since you will probably not know every term listed and the answer to every question, it is important that you get credit for the ones that you do know. Don't miss any questions through careless mistakes. If at all possible, try to take a second to look back over your answer selection and make sure you've selected the correct answer choice and haven't made a costly careless mistake (such as marking an answer choice that you didn't mean to mark). This quick double check should more than pay for itself in caught mistakes for the time it costs.

Beware of Directly Quoted Answers

Sometimes an answer choice will repeat word for word a portion of the question or reference section. However, beware of such exact duplication – it may be a trap! More than likely, the correct choice will paraphrase or summarize a point, rather than being exactly the same wording.

Slang

Scientific sounding answers are better than slang ones. An answer choice that begins "To compare the outcomes..." is much more likely to be correct than one that begins "Because some people insisted..."

Extreme Statements

Avoid wild answers that throw out highly controversial ideas that are proclaimed as established fact. An answer choice that states the "process should be used in certain situations, if..." is much more likely to be correct than one that states the "process should be discontinued completely." The first is a calm rational statement and doesn't even make a definitive, uncompromising stance, using a hedge word "if" to provide wiggle room, whereas the second choice is a radical idea and far more extreme.

Answer Choice Families

When you have two or more answer choices that are direct opposites or parallels, one of them is usually the correct answer. For instance, if one answer choice states "x increases" and another answer choice states "x decreases" or "y increases," then those two or three answer choices are very similar in construction and fall into the same family of answer choices. A family of answer choices is when two or three answer choices are very similar in construction, and yet often have a directly opposite meaning. Usually the correct answer choice will be in that family of answer choices. The "odd man out" or answer choice that doesn't seem to fit the parallel construction of the other answer choices is more likely to be incorrect.

Special Report: What Your Test Score Will Tell You About Your IQ

Did you know that most standardized tests correlate very strongly with IQ? In fact, your general intelligence is a better predictor of your success than any other factor, and most tests intentionally measure this trait to some degree to ensure that those selected by the test are truly qualified for the test's purposes.

Before we can delve into the relation between your test score and IQ, I will first have to explain what exactly is IQ. Here's the formula:

Your IQ = 100 + (Number of standard deviations below or above the average)*15

Now, let's define standard deviations by using an example. If we have 5 people with 5 different heights, then first we calculate the average. Let's say the average was 65 inches. The standard deviation is the "average distance" away from the average of each of the members. It is a direct measure of variability - if the 5 people included Jackie Chan and Shaquille O'Neal, obviously there's a lot more variability in that group than a group of 5 sisters who are all within 6 inches in height of each other. The standard deviation uses a number to characterize the average range of difference within a group.

A convenient feature of most groups is that they have a "normal" distribution- makes sense that most things would be normal, right? Without getting into a bunch of statistical mumbo-jumbo, you just need to know that if you know the average of the group and the standard deviation, you can successfully predict someone's percentile rank in the group.

Confused? Let me give you an example. If instead of 5 people's heights, we had 100 people, we could figure out their rank in height JUST by knowing the average, standard deviation, and their height. We wouldn't need to know each person's height and manually rank them, we could just predict their rank based on three numbers.

What this means is that you can take your PERCENTILE rank that is often given with your test and relate this to your RELATIVE IQ of people taking the test - that is, your IQ relative to the people taking the test. Obviously, there's no way to know your actual IQ because the people taking a standardized test are usually not very good samples of the general population- many of those with extremely low IQ's never achieve a level of success or competency necessary to complete a typical standardized test. In fact, professional psychologists who measure IQ actually have to use non-written tests that can fairly measure the IQ of those not able to complete a traditional test.

The bottom line is to not take your test score too seriously, but it is fun to compute your "relative IQ" among the people who took the test with you. I've done the calculations below. Just look up your percentile rank in the left and then you'll see your "relative IQ" for your test in the right hand column-

Percentile Rank	Your Relative IQ		Percentile Rank	Your Relative IQ
99	135		59	103
98	131		58	103
97	128		57	103
96	126		56	102
95	125		55	102
94	123		54	102
93	122		53	101
92	121		52	101
91	120		51	100
90	119		50	100
89	118		49	100
88	118		48	99
87	117		47	99
86	116		46	98
85	116		45	98
84	115		44	98
83	114		43	97
82	114		42	97
81	113		41	97
80	113		40	96
79	112		39	96
78	112		38	95
77	111		37	95
76	111		36	95
75	110		35	94
74	110		34	94
73	109		33	93
72	109		32	93
71	108		31	93
70	108		30	92
69	107		29	92
68	107		28	91
67	107		27	91
66	106		26	90
65	106		25	90
64	105		24	89
63	105		23	89
62	105		22	88
61	104		21	88
60	104		20	87

Special Report: What is Test Anxiety and How to Overcome It?

The very nature of tests caters to some level of anxiety, nervousness or tension, just as we feel for any important event that occurs in our lives. A little bit of anxiety or nervousness can be a good thing. It helps us with motivation, and makes achievement just that much sweeter. However, too much anxiety can be a problem; especially if it hinders our ability to function and perform.

"Test anxiety," is the term that refers to the emotional reactions that some test-takers experience when faced with a test or exam. Having a fear of testing and exams is based upon a rational fear, since the test-taker's performance can shape the course of an academic career. Nevertheless, experiencing excessive fear of examinations will only interfere with the test-takers ability to perform, and his/her chances to be successful.

There are a large variety of causes that can contribute to the development and sensation of test anxiety. These include, but are not limited to lack of performance and worrying about issues surrounding the test.

Lack of Preparation

Lack of preparation can be identified by the following behaviors or situations:
- Not scheduling enough time to study, and therefore cramming the night before the test or exam
- Managing time poorly, to create the sensation that there is not enough time to do everything
- Failing to organize the text information in advance, so that the study material consists of the entire text and not simply the pertinent information
- Poor overall studying habits

Worrying, on the other hand, can be related to both the test taker, or many other factors around him/her that will be affected by the results of the test. These include worrying about:
- Previous performances on similar exams, or exams in general
- How friends and other students are achieving
- The negative consequences that will result from a poor grade or failure

There are three primary elements to test anxiety. Physical components, which involve the same typical bodily reactions as those to acute anxiety (to be discussed below). Emotional factors have to do with fear or panic. Mental or cognitive issues concerning attention spans and memory abilities.

Physical Signals

There are many different symptoms of test anxiety, and these are not limited to mental and emotional strain. Frequently there are a range of physical signals that will let a test taker know that he/she is suffering from test anxiety. These bodily changes can include the following:

- Perspiring
- Sweaty palms
- Wet, trembling hands
- Nausea
- Dry mouth
- A knot in the stomach
- Headache
- Faintness
- Muscle tension
- Aching shoulders, back and neck
- Rapid heart beat
- Feeling too hot/cold

To recognize the sensation of test anxiety, a test-taker should monitor him/herself for the following sensations:

- The physical distress symptoms as listed above
- Emotional sensitivity, expressing emotional feelings such as the need to cry or laugh too much, or a sensation of anger or helplessness
- A decreased ability to think, causing the test-taker to blank out or have racing thoughts that are hard to organize or control.

Though most students will feel some level of anxiety when faced with a test or exam, the majority can cope with that anxiety and maintain it at a manageable level. However, those who cannot are faced with a very real and very serious condition, which can and should be controlled for the immeasurable benefit of this sufferer.

Naturally, these sensations lead to negative results for the testing experience. The most common effects of test anxiety have to do with nervousness and mental blocking.

Nervousness

Nervousness can appear in several different levels:

- The test-taker's difficulty, or even inability to read and understand the questions on the test
- The difficulty or inability to organize thoughts to a coherent form
- The difficulty or inability to recall key words and concepts relating to the testing questions (especially essays)
- The receipt of poor grades on a test, though the test material was well known by the test taker

Conversely, a person may also experience mental blocking, which involves:

- Blanking out on test questions
- Only remembering the correct answers to the questions when the test has already finished.

Fortunately for test anxiety sufferers, beating these feelings, to a large degree, has to do with proper preparation. When a test taker has a feeling of preparedness, then anxiety will be dramatically lessened.

The first step to resolving anxiety issues is to distinguish which of the two types of anxiety are being suffered. If the anxiety is a direct result of a lack of preparation, this should be considered a normal reaction, and the anxiety level (as opposed to the test results) shouldn't be anything to worry about. However, if, when adequately prepared, the test-taker still panics, blanks out, or seems to overreact, this is not a fully rational reaction. While this can be considered normal too, there are many ways to combat and overcome these effects.

Remember that anxiety cannot be entirely eliminated, however, there are ways to minimize it, to make the anxiety easier to manage. Preparation is one of the best ways to minimize test anxiety. Therefore the following techniques are wise in order to best fight off any anxiety that may want to build.

To begin with, try to avoid cramming before a test, whenever it is possible. By trying to memorize an entire term's worth of information in one day, you'll be shocking your system, and not giving yourself a very good chance to absorb the information. This is an easy path to anxiety, so for those who suffer from test anxiety, cramming should not even be considered an option.

Instead of cramming, work throughout the semester to combine all of the material which is presented throughout the semester, and work on it gradually as the course goes by, making sure to master the main concepts first, leaving minor details for a week or so before the test.

To study for the upcoming exam, be sure to pose questions that may be on the examination, to gauge the ability to answer them by integrating the ideas from your texts, notes and lectures, as well as any supplementary readings.

If it is truly impossible to cover all of the information that was covered in that particular term, concentrate on the most important portions, that can be covered very well. Learn these concepts as best as possible, so that when the test comes, a goal can be made to use these concepts as presentations of your knowledge.

In addition to study habits, changes in attitude are critical to beating a struggle with test anxiety. In fact, an improvement of the perspective over the entire test-taking experience can actually help a test taker to enjoy studying and therefore improve the overall experience. Be certain not to overemphasize the significance of the grade - know that the result of the test is neither a reflection of self worth, nor is it a measure of intelligence; one grade will not predict a person's future success.

To improve an overall testing outlook, the following steps should be tried:
- Keeping in mind that the most reasonable expectation for taking a test is to expect to try to demonstrate as much of what you know as you possibly can.
- Reminding ourselves that a test is only one test; this is not the only one, and there will be others.
- The thought of thinking of oneself in an irrational, all-or-nothing term should be avoided at all costs.
- A reward should be designated for after the test, so there's something to look forward to. Whether it be going to a movie, going out to eat, or simply visiting friends, schedule it in advance, and do it no matter what result is expected on the exam.

Test-takers should also keep in mind that the basics are some of the most important things, even beyond anti-anxiety techniques and studying. Never neglect the basic social, emotional and biological needs, in order to try to absorb information. In order to best achieve, these three factors must be held as just as important as the studying itself.

Study Steps

Remember the following important steps for studying:
- Maintain healthy nutrition and exercise habits. Continue both your recreational activities and social pass times. These both contribute to your physical and emotional well being.
- Be certain to get a good amount of sleep, especially the night before the test, because when you're overtired you are not able to perform to the best of your best ability.
- Keep the studying pace to a moderate level by taking breaks when they are needed, and varying the work whenever possible, to keep the mind fresh instead of getting bored.
- When enough studying has been done that all the material that can be learned has been learned, and the test taker is prepared for the test, stop studying and do something relaxing such as listening to music, watching a movie, or taking a warm bubble bath.

There are also many other techniques to minimize the uneasiness or apprehension that is experienced along with test anxiety before, during, or even after the examination. In fact, there are a great deal of things that can be done to stop anxiety from interfering with lifestyle and performance. Again, remember that anxiety will not be eliminated entirely, and it shouldn't be. Otherwise that "up" feeling for exams would not exist, and most of us depend on that sensation to perform better than usual. However, this anxiety has to be at a level that is manageable.

Of course, as we have just discussed, being prepared for the exam is half the battle right away. Attending all classes, finding out what knowledge will be expected on the exam, and knowing the exam schedules are easy steps to lowering anxiety. Keeping up with work will remove the need to cram, and efficient study habits will eliminate wasted time. Studying should be done in an ideal location for concentration, so that it is simple to become interested in the material and give it complete attention. A method such as

SQ3R (Survey, Question, Read, Recite, Review) is a wonderful key to follow to make sure that the study habits are as effective as possible, especially in the case of learning from a textbook. Flashcards are great techniques for memorization. Learning to take good notes will mean that notes will be full of useful information, so that less sifting will need to be done to seek out what is pertinent for studying. Reviewing notes after class and then again on occasion will keep the information fresh in the mind. From notes that have been taken summary sheets and outlines can be made for simpler reviewing.

A study group can also be a very motivational and helpful place to study, as there will be a sharing of ideas, all of the minds can work together, to make sure that everyone understands, and the studying will be made more interesting because it will be a social occasion.

Basically, though, as long as the test-taker remains organized and self confident, with efficient study habits, less time will need to be spent studying, and higher grades will be achieved.

To become self confident, there are many useful steps. The first of these is "self talk." It has been shown through extensive research, that self-talk for students who suffer from test anxiety, should be well monitored, in order to make sure that it contributes to self confidence as opposed to sinking the student. Frequently the self talk of test-anxious students is negative or self-defeating, thinking that everyone else is smarter and faster, that they always mess up, and that if they don't do well, they'll fail the entire course. It is important to decreasing anxiety that awareness is made of self talk. Try writing any negative self thoughts and then disputing them with a positive statement instead. Begin self-encouragement as though it was a friend speaking. Repeat positive statements to help reprogram the mind to believing in successes instead of failures.

Helpful Techniques

Other extremely helpful techniques include:
- Self-visualization of doing well and reaching goals
- While aiming for an "A" level of understanding, don't try to "overprotect" by setting your expectations lower. This will only convince the mind to stop studying in order to meet the lower expectations.
- Don't make comparisons with the results or habits of other students. These are individual factors, and different things work for different people, causing different results.
- Strive to become an expert in learning what works well, and what can be done in order to improve. Consider collecting this data in a journal.
- Create rewards for after studying instead of doing things before studying that will only turn into avoidance behaviors.
- Make a practice of relaxing - by using methods such as progressive relaxation, self-hypnosis, guided imagery, etc - in order to make relaxation an automatic sensation.
- Work on creating a state of relaxed concentration so that concentrating will take on the focus of the mind, so that none will be wasted on worrying.
- Take good care of the physical self by eating well and getting enough sleep.

- Plan in time for exercise and stick to this plan.

Beyond these techniques, there are other methods to be used before, during and after the test that will help the test-taker perform well in addition to overcoming anxiety.

Before the exam comes the academic preparation. This involves establishing a study schedule and beginning at least one week before the actual date of the test. By doing this, the anxiety of not having enough time to study for the test will be automatically eliminated. Moreover, this will make the studying a much more effective experience, ensuring that the learning will be an easier process. This relieves much undue pressure on the test-taker.

Summary sheets, note cards, and flash cards with the main concepts and examples of these main concepts should be prepared in advance of the actual studying time. A topic should never be eliminated from this process. By omitting a topic because it isn't expected to be on the test is only setting up the test-taker for anxiety should it actually appear on the exam. Utilize the course syllabus for laying out the topics that should be studied. Carefully go over the notes that were made in class, paying special attention to any of the issues that the professor took special care to emphasize while lecturing in class. In the textbooks, use the chapter review, or if possible, the chapter tests, to begin your review.

It may even be possible to ask the instructor what information will be covered on the exam, or what the format of the exam will be (for example, multiple choice, essay, free form, true-false). Additionally, see if it is possible to find out how many questions will be on the test. If a review sheet or sample test has been offered by the professor, make good use of it, above anything else, for the preparation for the test. Another great resource for getting to know the examination is reviewing tests from previous semesters. Use these tests to review, and aim to achieve a 100% score on each of the possible topics. With a few exceptions, the goal that you set for yourself is the highest one that you will reach.

Take all of the questions that were assigned as homework, and rework them to any other possible course material. The more problems reworked, the more skill and confidence will form as a result. When forming the solution to a problem, write out each of the steps. Don't simply do head work. By doing as many steps on paper as possible, much clarification and therefore confidence will be formed. Do this with as many homework problems as possible, before checking the answers. By checking the answer after each problem, a reinforcement will exist, that will not be on the exam. Study situations should be as exam-like as possible, to prime the test-taker's system for the experience. By waiting to check the answers at the end, a psychological advantage will be formed, to decrease the stress factor.

Another fantastic reason for not cramming is the avoidance of confusion in concepts, especially when it comes to mathematics. 8-10 hours of study will become one hundred percent more effective if it is spread out over a week or at least several days, instead of doing it all in one sitting. Recognize that the human brain requires time in order to assimilate new material, so frequent breaks and a span of study time over several days will be much more beneficial.

Additionally, don't study right up until the point of the exam. Studying should stop a minimum of one hour before the exam begins. This allows the brain to rest and put things in their proper order. This will also provide the time to become as relaxed as possible when going into the examination room. The test-taker will also have time to eat well and eat sensibly. Know that the brain needs food as much as the rest of the body. With enough food and enough sleep, as well as a relaxed attitude, the body and the mind are primed for success.

Avoid any anxious classmates who are talking about the exam. These students only spread anxiety, and are not worth sharing the anxious sentimentalities.

Before the test also involves creating a positive attitude, so mental preparation should also be a point of concentration. There are many keys to creating a positive attitude. Should fears become rushing in, make a visualization of taking the exam, doing well, and seeing an A written on the paper. Write out a list of affirmations that will bring a feeling of confidence, such as "I am doing well in my English class," "I studied well and know my material," "I enjoy this class." Even if the affirmations aren't believed at first, it sends a positive message to the subconscious which will result in an alteration of the overall belief system, which is the system that creates reality.

If a sensation of panic begins, work with the fear and imagine the very worst! Work through the entire scenario of not passing the test, failing the entire course, and dropping out of school, followed by not getting a job, and pushing a shopping cart through the dark alley where you'll live. This will place things into perspective! Then, practice deep breathing and create a visualization of the opposite situation - achieving an "A" on the exam, passing the entire course, receiving the degree at a graduation ceremony.

On the day of the test, there are many things to be done to ensure the best results, as well as the most calm outlook. The following stages are suggested in order to maximize test-taking potential:

- Begin the examination day with a moderate breakfast, and avoid any coffee or beverages with caffeine if the test taker is prone to jitters. Even people who are used to managing caffeine can feel jittery or light-headed when it is taken on a test day.
- Attempt to do something that is relaxing before the examination begins. As last minute cramming clouds the mastering of overall concepts, it is better to use this time to create a calming outlook.
- Be certain to arrive at the test location well in advance, in order to provide time to select a location that is away from doors, windows and other distractions, as well as giving enough time to relax before the test begins.
- Keep away from anxiety generating classmates who will upset the sensation of stability and relaxation that is being attempted before the exam.
- Should the waiting period before the exam begins cause anxiety, create a self-distraction by reading a light magazine or something else that is relaxing and simple.

During the exam itself, read the entire exam from beginning to end, and find out how much time should be allotted to each individual problem. Once writing the exam, should more time be taken for a problem, it should be abandoned, in order to begin another problem. If there is time at the end, the unfinished problem can always be returned to and completed.

Read the instructions very carefully - twice - so that unpleasant surprises won't follow during or after the exam has ended.

When writing the exam, pretend that the situation is actually simply the completion of homework within a library, or at home. This will assist in forming a relaxed atmosphere, and will allow the brain extra focus for the complex thinking function.

Begin the exam with all of the questions with which the most confidence is felt. This will build the confidence level regarding the entire exam and will begin a quality momentum. This will also create encouragement for trying the problems where uncertainty resides.

Going with the "gut instinct" is always the way to go when solving a problem. Second guessing should be avoided at all costs. Have confidence in the ability to do well.

For essay questions, create an outline in advance that will keep the mind organized and make certain that all of the points are remembered. For multiple choice, read every answer, even if the correct one has been spotted - a better one may exist.

Continue at a pace that is reasonable and not rushed, in order to be able to work carefully. Provide enough time to go over the answers at the end, to check for small errors that can be corrected.

Should a feeling of panic begin, breathe deeply, and think of the feeling of the body releasing sand through its pores. Visualize a calm, peaceful place, and include all of the sights, sounds and sensations of this image. Continue the deep breathing, and take a few minutes to continue this with closed eyes. When all is well again, return to the test.

If a "blanking" occurs for a certain question, skip it and move on to the next question. There will be time to return to the other question later. Get everything done that can be done, first, to guarantee all the grades that can be compiled, and to build all of the confidence possible. Then return to the weaker questions to build the marks from there.

Remember, one's own reality can be created, so as long as the belief is there, success will follow. And remember: anxiety can happen later, right now, there's an exam to be written!

After the examination is complete, whether there is a feeling for a good grade or a bad grade, don't dwell on the exam, and be certain to follow through on the reward that was promised...and enjoy it! Don't dwell on any mistakes that have been made, as there is nothing that can be done at this point anyway.

Additionally, don't begin to study for the next test right away. Do something relaxing for a while, and let the mind relax and prepare itself to begin absorbing information again.

From the results of the exam - both the grade and the entire experience, be certain to learn from what has gone on. Perfect studying habits and work some more on confidence in order to make the next examination experience even better than the last one.

Learn to avoid places where openings occurred for laziness, procrastination and day dreaming.

Use the time between this exam and the next one to better learn to relax, even learning to relax on cue, so that any anxiety can be controlled during the next exam. Learn how to relax the body. Slouch in your chair if that helps. Tighten and then relax all of the different muscle groups, one group at a time, beginning with the feet and then working all the way up to the neck and face. This will ultimately relax the muscles more than they were to begin with. Learn how to breathe deeply and comfortably, and focus on this breathing going in and out as a relaxing thought. With every exhale, repeat the word "relax."

As common as test anxiety is, it is very possible to overcome it. Make yourself one of the test-takers who overcome this frustrating hindrance.

Special Report: Retaking the Test: What Are Your Chances at Improving Your Score?

After going through the experience of taking a major test, many test takers feel that once is enough. The test usually comes during a period of transition in the test taker's life, and taking the test is only one of a series of important events. With so many distractions and conflicting recommendations, it may be difficult for a test taker to rationally determine whether or not he should retake the test after viewing his scores.

The importance of the test usually only adds to the burden of the retake decision. However, don't be swayed by emotion. There a few simple questions that you can ask yourself to guide you as you try to determine whether a retake would improve your score:

1. What went wrong? Why wasn't your score what you expected?

Can you point to a single factor or problem that you feel caused the low score? Were you sick on test day? Was there an emotional upheaval in your life that caused a distraction? Were you late for the test or not able to use the full time allotment? If you can point to any of these specific, individual problems, then a retake should definitely be considered.

2. Is there enough time to improve?

Many problems that may show up in your score report may take a lot of time for improvement. A deficiency in a particular math skill may require weeks or months of tutoring and studying to improve. If you have enough time to improve an identified weakness, then a retake should definitely be considered.

3. How will additional scores be used? Will a score average, highest score, or most recent score be used?

Different test scores may be handled completely differently. If you've taken the test multiple times, sometimes your highest score is used, sometimes your average score is computed and used, and sometimes your most recent score is used. Make sure you understand what method will be used to evaluate your scores, and use that to help you determine whether a retake should be considered.

4. Are my practice test scores significantly higher than my actual test score?

If you have taken a lot of practice tests and are consistently scoring at a much higher level than your actual test score, then you should consider a retake. However, if you've taken five practice tests and only one of your scores was higher than your actual test score, or if your practice test scores were only slightly higher than your actual test score, then it is unlikely that you will significantly increase your score.

5. Do I need perfect scores or will I be able to live with this score? Will this score still allow me to follow my dreams?

What kind of score is acceptable to you? Is your current score "good enough?" Do you have to have a certain score in order to pursue the future of your dreams? If you won't be happy with your current score, and there's no way that you could live with it, then you should consider a retake. However, don't get your hopes up. If you are looking for significant improvement, that may or may not be possible. But if you won't be happy otherwise, it is at least worth the effort.

Remember that there are other considerations. To achieve your dream, it is likely that your grades may also be taken into account. A great test score is usually not the only thing necessary to succeed. Make sure that you aren't overemphasizing the importance of a high test score.

Furthermore, a retake does not always result in a higher score. Some test takers will score lower on a retake, rather than higher. One study shows that one-fourth of test takers will achieve a significant improvement in test score, while one-sixth of test takers will actually show a decrease. While this shows that most test takers will improve, the majority will only improve their scores a little and a retake may not be worth the test taker's effort.

Finally, if a test is taken only once and is considered in the added context of good grades on the part of a test taker, the person reviewing the grades and scores may be tempted to assume that the test taker just had a bad day while taking the test, and may discount the low test score in favor of the high grades. But if the test is retaken and the scores are approximately the same, then the validity of the low scores are only confirmed. Therefore, a retake could actually hurt a test taker by definitely bracketing a test taker's score ability to a limited range.